SPOOKY
South

Also in the Spooky Series by S. E. Schlosser and Paul G. Hoffman

Spooky Appalachia
Spooky California
Spooky Campfire Tales
Spooky Canada
Spooky Christmas
Spooky Colorado
Spooky Florida
Spooky Georgia
Spooky Great Lakes
Spooky Great Smokies
Spooky Indiana
Spooky Maryland
Spooky Massachusetts
Spooky Michigan
Spooky Montana
Spooky New England
Spooky New Jersey
Spooky New Orleans
Spooky New York
Spooky North Carolina
Spooky Ohio
Spooky Oregon
Spooky Pennsylvania
Spooky Southwest
Spooky Tennessee
Spooky Texas
Spooky Virginia
Spooky Washington
Spooky Wisconsin
Spooky Yellowstone

SPOOKY
South

Tales of Hauntings, Strange Happenings,
and Other Local Lore

THIRD EDITION

RETOLD BY S. E. SCHLOSSER
ILLUSTRATED BY PAUL G. HOFFMAN

Globe
Pequot
ESSEX, CONNECTICUT

Globe
Pequot

An imprint of Globe Pequot, the trade division of
The Rowman & Littlefield Publishing Group, Inc.
4501 Forbes Blvd., Ste. 200
Lanham, MD 20706
www.rowman.com

Distributed by NATIONAL BOOK NETWORK

British Library Cataloguing in Publication Information available

Library of Congress Cataloging-in-Publication Data
Names: Schlosser, S. E., author. | Hoffman, Paul G., illustrator.
Title: Spooky South : tales of hauntings, strange happenings, and other local
  lore / retold by S. E. Schlosser ; illustrated by Paul G. Hoffman.
Description: Third edition. | Essex, Connecticut : Globe Pequot, [2024] |
  Series: Spooky series | Includes bibliographical references.
Identifiers: LCCN 2024012030 (print) | LCCN 2024012031 (ebook) |
  ISBN 9781493069903 (paperback) | ISBN 9781493069910 (epub)
Subjects: LCSH: Ghosts—Southern States. | Haunted places—Southern
  States.
Classification: LCC BF1472.U6 S329 2024 (print) | LCC BF1472.U6
  (ebook) | DDC 133.10975—dc23/eng/20240424
LC record available at https://lccn.loc.gov/2024012030
LC ebook record available at https://lccn.loc.gov/2024012031

For my family: David, Dena, Tim, Arlene, Hannah, Seth, Theo, Rory, Emma, Nathan, Ben, Karen, Davey, Deb, Gabe, Clare, Jack, and Chris.

For Aunt Millie, who faithfully read stories to all her nieces and nephews, and for Aunt Lynetta and Uncle John, who took us used book shopping.

For Coley, whose favorite Spooky Story is Chattanooga's Ghost.

For all my relatives who are smart enough to live in the South: Liz, Rich, Steven, Dan, Kirsten, Anne, Nathaniel, Melinda, Elizabeth, and Hannah.

Contents

Contents

Contents

SPOOKY SITES . . .

①	Kanawha County, WV	㉓	Knoxville, TN
②	Red River Landing, LA	㉔	Guilford County, NC
③	Camden, SC	㉕	Great Dismal Swamp, VA
④	Charleston, SC	㉖	New Orleans, LA
⑤	Raleigh County, WV	㉗	Wheeler National Wildlife Refuge, AL
⑥	Sea Island, GA		
⑦	Madison, NC	㉘	Harrison County, MS
⑧	Birmingham, AL	㉙	St. Augustine, FL
⑨	New Orleans, LA	㉚	Albright, WV
⑩	Hampton, VA	㉛	Montgomery County, TN
⑪	Berlin, MD	㉜	New Orleans, LA
⑫	Greenville, MS	㉝	Maryville, TN
⑬	Ocracoke Inlet, NC	㉞	Richmond, VA
⑭	Montgomery County, AR	㉟	Tombigbee Region, AL
⑮	Savannah, GA	㊱	Daytona Beach, FL
⑯	Goldsboro, NC	㊲	Jacksonville, FL
⑰	Brunswick, GA	㊳	Bentonville, AR
⑱	Dukedom, TN	㊴	Adams, TN
⑲	Hiawassee, GA	㊵	Big Stone Gap, VA
⑳	Allegany County, MD	㊶	Summersville, WV
㉑	Pensacola, FL	㊷	Easton, MD
㉒	Mount Pleasant, SC	㊸	Beaufort, SC

AND WHERE TO FIND THEM

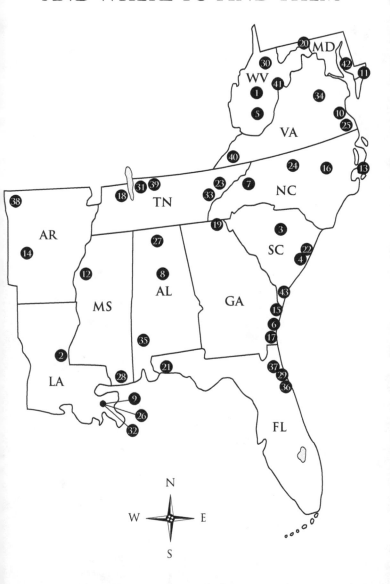

Introduction

The beach sand gleamed irresistibly in the late winter sun, and I was quick to slide off my shoes and push my toes into the chilly, glittering granules. Bliss.

The day was warm; the breeze slight; and the beach empty of visitors. I joyfully locked my winter jacket in the car and started up the sandy path, my precious DSLR clutched in my hands. My feet worked harder than usual in the shifting sand, but I didn't care. This was sheer heaven after the bleak snow and ice of the North.

My mission that day was simple; photograph a picturesque, abandoned lighthouse and then head over for a tour of a nearby haunted plantation. Lighthouses are a hobby of mine. Whenever a spooky research trip brings me in the vicinity of a lighthouse, I inevitably find myself aimed in its direction.

My quarry became visible as I topped a small sand dune; its red and white stripes angled in a continuous spiral down its length. To add more pathos to the heart-catching scene, a pair of bottlenose dolphins played in the surf before it. To my left, driftwood trees formed natural sculptures in the sand. To my right, a stone seawall thrust itself out into the waves. I raised my camera, not sure what to photograph first among so many wonders.

Many pictures later, I sat down on the sea wall to breathe in the crisp, salty air and think about my journey so far through the spooky South with its many ghosts; quite a number of which were associated with the sea. In Ocracoke Inlet, North Carolina, the pirate Edward Teach roams the beach looking for his lost head (Blackbeard's Ghost). Further south, the Sea Islanders of Georgia still use an old spell to help them get in contact with the spirits (Seeing Ghosts). And down in Brunswick Georgia, a lonely ghost tries to lure family members into the waters of the inlet to join her in death (I Know Moonrise).

The sea was not the only body of water to produce ghosts. The swamplands and rivers of the South have their fair share of haunts as well. Down in New Orleans, an old roustabout refuses to go to heaven until he's smoked every last one of his expensive cigars (Chattanooga's Ghost). In Greenville Mississippi, a drowning victim haunts an old drunk until he promises to lay off the booze (The Waves Call). Over in the Great Dismal Swamp of Virginia, Goggle-Eyed Jim keeps stealing horses long after he's dead. And in Hiawassee Georgia, the phantom of a native warrior drives a grave robber into a flooded river at the height of a storm (The Dead Chief).

On land, spirits haunt mountain and valley, and all the places in between. In Charleston South Carolina, the Army of the Dead nightly roams the streets, on their way to reinforce General Lee's troops in Virginia. Over in Berlin, Maryland, a ghost hides a runaway slave who gets into trouble on his way to catch Harriet Tubman's Glory Train (Steal Away Home). And in Birmingham Alabama, a sports-obsessed man gets into trouble with a ghost one night after staying out late to watch his home team defeat their rivals (The Baseball Game).

I glanced at my watch and reluctantly realized that it was time to head back to the car. "I wonder what ghosts might be lurking unnoticed on my plantation tour this afternoon," I said to a greedy sea gull trolling for leftovers. "If any of them come scratch-scratch-scratching on the door like Tailypo, I'm out of here!" The sea gull fluffed its feathers in sympathy, as if it understood my every word. With a sigh of regret, I slid off the sea wall and headed toward the car.

At the top of the dune, I looked back toward the lighthouse and saw a glint at the top. My pulse quickened. Was that a glowing figure looking down at me from behind the glass? Or was it just a chance ray of sun? I blinked and the glint was gone. What had I just seen? I shivered in the warm sun, my arms all-over goose bumps. It was probably just a trick of the light. Or maybe not . . .

"This *is* the spooky South," I reminded myself as I sped hastily toward the parking lot. "Anything can happen here!"

Happy Hauntings.

—Sandy Schlosser

PART ONE
Ghost Stories

1

Wait Until Emmet Comes

KANAWHA COUNTY, WEST VIRGINIA

A preacher was riding to one of the churches on his circuit when darkness fell. It was about to storm and the only shelter around was an old, abandoned mansion, reputed to be haunted. The preacher clutched his Bible and said, "The Lord will take care o' me."

The preacher arrived at the mansion just as the storm broke. He put his horse in the barn and made his way to the house. The front door was unlocked. He entered a gloomy old hallway and looked into the first room on his left. It was a large room, with a huge fireplace that filled one entire wall. Coal for a fire had been laid in the fireplace, and several comfortable chairs were grouped invitingly around the hearth. Surprised to find such a pleasant room in an abandoned house, the preacher went in and set a match to light the fire, then he settled down in one of the comfortable chairs and began to read his Bible.

The fire smoldered in a heap of glowing coals as the storm howled around the mansion and shook the windows. Roused from his reading by a noise, the preacher looked up from his Bible. A very large black cat was stretching itself in the doorway. It walked to the fire and sat down among the red-hot coals. The

WAIT UNTIL EMMET COMES

preacher swallowed nervously as the cat picked up a coal in its paw and licked it. Then the cat got up, shook itself, and walked to the foot of the preacher's chair. It fixed its blazing yellow eyes on the preacher, black tail lashing, and said quietly, "Wait until Emmet comes."

The preacher jumped from Genesis to Matthew in shock. He had never heard of a talking cat before. The cat sat down in front of the preacher and watched him without blinking. The preacher turned back to his Bible, nervously muttering to himself, "The Lord will take care o' me."

Two minutes later, another cat came into the room. It was black as midnight and as large as the biggest dog you've ever seen. It laid down among the red-hot coals, lazily batting them with its enormous paws. Then it walked over to the first cat and said, "What shall we do with him?"

The cat replied, "We should not do anything until Emmet comes."

The two cats sat facing the chair, watching as the preacher read through the Gospels at top speed. Their blazing yellow eyes seemed never to blink.

A third black cat, big as a tiger, entered the room. It went to the fireplace full of red-hot coals and rolled among them, chewing some and spitting them out. Then it ambled over to the other two cats that were facing the preacher in his chair.

"What shall we do with him?" it growled to the others.

"We should not do anything until Emmet comes," the cats replied together.

The preacher flipped to Revelation, looking fearfully around the room. Then he snapped shut his Bible and stood up.

"Goodnight cats," he said politely. "I'm glad of your company, but when Emmet comes, you done tell him I've been here . . . and gone!"

2

The Cut-Off

The Mississippi River was an unsettled and uneasy place to be that night. You could feel the tension rising every time the water swirled and slapped against the side of the boat or the warning bell jangled. The light of the lantern barely penetrated the enveloping fog, and the engine chugged and strained. It was a bad night to be out in a paddleboat. But the pilot had sworn when he set out that nothing would make him turn back.

No other pilot dared to brave the Mississippi that night. They were all huddled in the tavern, gossiping and telling tales. After an evening spent listening to empty boasts, the pilot had made one himself. He said he knew the Mississippi River so well that he could guide his paddleboat through the thickness of the night fog. The other pilots laughed and told him he would be back before midnight. He had grown angry at their jeers and had sworn to them he would not turn back for any reason, should the devil bar the way!

The pilot jerked the wheel, anger filling him again at the memory of their laughter. The paddleboat shuddered. He pulled himself together and straightened the boat. It was difficult

THE CUT-OFF

enough piloting in the dense fog without adding carelessness to the mix of dangers.

The paddleboat was rocking oddly under the strange eddies of the river, but the pilot knew every turn and guided the paddleboat along despite the fog. Occasionally, he could make out the dark shape of an island or a flicker of light from the shore, encouraging him onward.

He turned down a familiar bend and was nearly through the channel when he saw shore where no shore had ever been before. He slowed the paddleboat, turning it this way and that. It could not be! The river ran straight through this branch. He had guided his paddleboat through this place a hundred times.

But the Mississippi had shifted. Unbeknownst to the pilot, a new cut-off had been made just below Red River Landing. Already the old channel into which he had piloted his paddleboat was beginning to fill with reefs and debris.

The pilot swore every curse he knew and kept searching for a way through. Surely there was still an opening somewhere. He had vowed to complete his run without turning back, and he was determined to fulfill his promise. He would never go back. Never! He would stay there until daybreak, and beyond if need be.

Edging the boat forward through the fog, the pilot thought he could see a gleam of water ahead. It looked like an opening. He sped up, intent on breaking out of the now useless channel. Suddenly, the paddleboat gave a massive jerk and the engine stalled. He had hit something! The pilot started the engine and tried to back up. The engine wailed as he pulled away from the submerged obstacle. The paddleboat shuddered and started to list as water burst through the hull. Then it overturned, trapping the pilot underneath. He struggled to find a way out, but he could see nothing in the darkness. The boat sank rapidly beneath the water, taking the pilot with it.

When the fog lifted the next day, several of the boatmen, concerned by the pilot's continued absence, went in search of their friend. They found his paddleboat sunk to the bottom with a gaping hole in its side and the pilot drowned.

A month later, a riverboat captain was trying to beat the fog into Red River Landing when he heard the ring of a bell and the sound of a paddleboat engine coming from the old channel. Curious, he stilled his engine to listen. In the eerie silence that followed, he distinctly heard a voice cursing loudly over the chugging of a paddleboat engine. Was that a ghostly apparition of the pilot trying to force his way through the blocked channel?! Frightened, the captain hurried into Red River Landing and went to the local tavern to drink away his scare. The bartender laughed at his tale of the phantom paddleboat and sent him home to sleep it off. But it was not long after this that other pilots began hearing the phantom paddleboat on foggy nights, as its ghostly pilot tried again and again to complete his run. The river near the old channel was avoided thereafter.

They say if you stand near the old channel on foggy nights, you can still hear the ring of the bell, the sound of the engine, and the curses of the ghost pilot trying to complete his run.

3

I'm Coming Down

Well, you've never heard a scary ghost story till you've heard my ghost story, no sir! I tell you, I've seen the creepiest ghost that ever walked this earth, or my name's not Big Jo Jo Boll Weevil Jim.

A few years back I spent a couple of weeks down in Charleston visiting my old mother. When I left Charleston I had a pocket full of money, but by the time I reached Camden, I found myself out of money and without a ride. I was still quite a piece from home, and I knew that I was going to have to walk the rest of the way. This was 'round about the fall of the year, and it was starting to get cold. As I hurried down the road, I wondered if I should try to locate my wife's second cousin Lulu, who lived near Camden. But I decided against it. First because I didn't know exactly where Lulu lived, and second because Lulu and I don't get along. I figured I could camp out that night and maybe catch me a fish or two to keep the hunger pangs away till I reached home. But then it started to rain, and I decided I needed to find a place to stay for the night.

So the first house I saw, I marched straight up to the door and knocked. A man came to the door and I explained to him

I'M COMING DOWN

what terrible straits I was in, and I asked him if he had a barn or a doghouse or something where I could stay the night. Well, the man took a good look at me, and I guess he decided I didn't mean no harm, 'cause he said he had a house up the hill where no one was living, and he reckoned it would be all right for me to fix up a fire and sleep in the bed.

This was a stroke of good luck. A fire and a bed sounded better than a doghouse or a stack of hay. I thanked him right quick and wished him goodnight. Then I went straight up the hill and into the little gray house I found there.

Now make no mistake, this was a nice house. Seemed a bit odd that no one wanted to live there, but I wasn't about to question my good fortune, no sir. I made me up a fire in the fireplace and set myself down to dry out. I was getting really warm and cozy when all at once I heard this voice a-coming from up the stairs. It was a deep voice, and it echoed around and around the house.

"I'm coming down!" the voice boomed.

Well sir, I jumped a mile. The man had said the house was deserted, and it sure had looked deserted when I got there. But now I was hearin' a voice that made my hair stand on end and gave me goose bumps. The voice didn't sound like anyone alive, if you know what I mean.

"I'm coming down!" the voice roared again.

It sounded closer this time, though it was hard to judge distance with the voice echoing all over the place. And then, sure enough, there was a man standing at the bottom of the stairs. He was dressed all in white and he glowed like someone had lit a candle inside his skin. There was something about the way his eyes looked at me that made me real sorry that he was standing between me and the door.

About then I reckoned a change of address would be good for my health, so I lit out the window and ran about seven miles down the road without stopping. I nearly knocked over the preacher on my way, and he yelled at me to halt. I glanced back but didn't see the man in white chasing me, so I stopped.

"Young man," said the preacher, "just where do you think you are going in such a hurry?"

"Preacher," says I, "if you'd just seen what I've just seen, you'd be in a hurry too."

Well the preacher insisted I tell him my story right then and there. So I did. And don't you know, that preacher, he started to laugh and said, "Friend, there's nothing to that."

"What you mean, nothing to that?" I was indignant. After all, it was me and not the preacher who saw that scary ghost.

"Listen, friend, we've got the Lord on our side, and we don't need to be scared of ghosts. I'll prove you were wrong."

"How?" I asked him.

"I'll go with you to the house," the preacher said.

"You and who else?" I asked him, 'cause I didn't want to see that scary ghost again, nohow.

"Me and the Lord, of course," said the preacher.

Well, I can't say as I was convinced that this was enough, but it's mighty hard to contradict a preacher. And my wife's second cousin Lulu went to the preacher's church, and I knew she would tell my wife if I insulted a man of God. So I went back to the house with the preacher. It was a long, long time before we got to the house. I'd run lickety-split when I saw that ghost, and I'd covered a lot of ground. But the light was still lit when we arrived, and the fire still burned cheerfully.

Well, the preacher walked right in, not scared a bit. I followed a bit slower, looking around for that man in white, but there was no sign of him. Just in case, I left the window open and made sure there was nothing blocking our way.

But the preacher, he just sat down by the fire. I took the other chair, mainly because it was closer to the window, and waited for the ghost to come.

Sure enough, a few minutes later the voice began booming from upstairs: "I'm coming down." My hair stood on end, my arms came out in goose bumps. I just looked at the preacher, and he just looked at me. The voice came again: "I'm coming down!"

And the man in white appeared at the bottom of the stairs. He was glowing from the inside, and his eyes blazed at me and the preacher. I didn't wait around to see the preacher take on that ghost, no sir. I lit out that window even faster than the first time. I reckoned the preacher and the Lord didn't need my help dealing with that ghost.

After a few minutes of serious sprinting, I realized that the preacher was running at my side. And boy could he run! He nearly passed me, and I had some trouble keeping up with him. After about ten miles, I yelled for the preacher to stop. There was no sign of that ghost, so the preacher stopped.

When I got my breath back, I asked the preacher if he thought that the good Lord was still with us.

"Well if He is," the preacher gasped, "then He must have been running real fast."

4

The Army of the Dead

Liza lay awake late into the night, her mind racing as she reviewed all the new sights, sounds, and smells she'd experienced that day in Charleston, where she and her husband had just set up house. The city was overwhelming compared to the small town where she and Johnny had been living up until now. Johnny had grown up in Charleston and was thrilled to be back. More than once he had pulled her away from the unpacking to show her a familiar place. He was nearly dancing with glee. Liza smiled, remembering his face. She glanced over at him, sleeping peacefully beside her, and finally she slept too.

Liza awoke suddenly, her heart pounding. Outside, she could hear the church bell tolling midnight, but it was not the toll of the bell that had wakened her. It was the rumble of heavy wagon wheels passing under her window that had jolted her from her sleep. But where were the wagons going? Their new house was on a dead-end street.

"Johnny," she hissed, shaking her husband's arm.

He mumbled and turned over.

"Johnny," she tried again. He opened his eyes and said, "What's the matter?"

THE ARMY OF THE DEAD

"Can't you hear the wagons?" she asked.

Johnny came awake immediately. He sat up, listening. Then he lay back down and said, "It's nothing. Go back to sleep."

"Nothing? It sounds like a whole wagon train is passing!" Liza sat up and moved to get out of bed.

"Don't!" her husband said sharply. "Do not ever look out the window when you hear those sounds."

Liza turned to look at Johnny. His voice sounded so strange, as if he were afraid.

"Get back in bed. Please," Johnny said. Now she was sure. Johnny was frightened. She got back into bed, but lay awake a long time after the sound of the passing wagons had ceased.

Liza started her new job at the laundry the next morning. The work was hard, but the other women were nice, and she quickly learned the routine. Within a few days, Liza was feeling comfortable in her new home. During the day, she gossiped with the other women as they washed the clothing. In the evenings, she and Johnny finished unpacking and discussed their new neighbors around the fireplace. But each night Liza was awakened at midnight by the rumble of wagons. Sometimes she thought she heard the sound of voices. They always passed close to her house, heading in the direction of the dead end. But when she walked down to the end of the street in the morning, there was no sign of people or wagons. Liza tried to talk to Johnny about the sounds, but he wouldn't say anything except to tell her to leave well enough alone, and to warn her not to look out the window when she heard the sounds.

After several weeks, Liza decided to ask Anna, the woman who washed at the tub next to hers, if she had ever heard the rumble of wagons late at night. Anna drew in a sharp breath when she heard the question and said, "What you are hearing is the Army of the Dead. They are Confederate soldiers who died without knowing the war was over. Each night, they rise from their graves and go to reinforce General Lee's troops in Virginia and shore up the Southern forces."

When Liza pressed Anna for details, her friend shook her head and would say no more. But she repeated Johnny's warning to leave well enough alone and not to look out the window.

That night, Liza lay awake, waiting for the bell to toll midnight. When she heard the first wagon wheels, she checked carefully to make sure Johnny was sleeping, and then she slipped out of bed. Pushing aside the thick curtain, Liza opened the window to watch the Army of the Dead.

Liza stood spellbound as a gray fog rolled passed. Within the fog she could make out the shapes of horses pulling large, heavily loaded wagons. She could hear gruff human voices and the rumble of cannons being dragged through the street. The wagons were followed by the sound of marching feet, and she saw foot soldiers, horsemen, and ambulances pass before her eyes, all shrouded in gray. After what seemed like hours, Liza heard a far-off bugle blast, and then silence. Slowly, the gray fog lifted and the moon came out.

Liza shook her head, suddenly aware of how cold and stiff she was. She stepped away from the window, wondering how long she had been watching. She stretched, but her right arm would not respond. She realized in sudden horror that she could not feel her arm at all. She gripped her right arm with her left hand and tried to move it. She was not aware of making a sound, but suddenly Johnny was beside her.

Liza gazed up at him mutely for a moment, trembling, and then managed to say, "Johnny. My arm . . . "

Johnny put his arm around her. He had taken in the situation at a glance, seeing the open window with the moonlight streaming inside. "Oh love, I am so sorry. I tried to warn you," he said softly. "There is a curse laid on anyone who watches the Army passing at night. Some people have lost limbs, some have lost their minds, and some have even lost their lives. The Army does not like to be watched."

Johnny prodded Liza's arm gently, but she could not feel a thing. Johnny put her arm into a sling, and the next day they saw a doctor, who confirmed that her arm was paralyzed.

After a month, partial feeling returned to Liza's arm, but she was never able to do a full day's washing again. And she never again got up to watch the Army of the Dead.

5

The Death Watch

Jim Kelly had dreaded this day for weeks. It was the first day of his new job, but it was a job he knew well. For fourteen years he had managed to escape the everlasting darkness, the dangers, the long climbs, and the narrow crawl spaces of the coal mines. Jim had hated the life of a coal miner. But with seven children to feed, he felt he had no choice but to return.

When Jim was thirteen his mother was widowed, and he went to work in a coal mine to help support his struggling family. But when Jim turned sixteen, his mother remarried a wealthy man. His new stepfather found Jim a place as a clerk in a store when he learned how Jim felt about mining.

Jim had done well at the store. He'd married his sweetheart Margaret when he was eighteen. They'd had seven children and bought a nice house in town, far away from the horrors of the coal mine. But then disaster struck in the form of a terrible fire that wiped out the entire town, leaving Jim without a home or a job.

Jim's youngest sister, Susan, took his family in until they could find another place to live, and Jeff, Jim's brother-in-law, got Jim a job working with him in the coal mine. Jim said the

THE DEATH WATCH

family was grateful to have a roof over their heads; still, he hated going back to mining. Margaret insisted it was only temporary. The town would be rebuilt, and Jim could go back to the store. Jim clung to that hope as he followed Jeff down the ladder into the darkness of the mine.

Jim had lost none of his mining skills, and he quickly settled into the daily routine. He stayed with Jeff for the first few days, working a coal seam, stooped over because the shaft was only five feet tall. All day they stood ankle deep in water, which constantly dripped from the ceiling. The conditions in this mine were just as miserable as in the mine where Jim had worked as a boy. But Jeff was a good companion, and he made that first week bearable with his friendly conversation. On the first day, Jeff told Jim the story of the death watch.

"Old Ted Miller was a bad one," Jeff said while they were taking a lunch break in the only dry space in the shaft they were working. "We always suspected he was stealing from the mine, but we never knew for sure until one day he was buried alive by a pillar of coal he was robbing. We dug his body out, but we couldn't find his watch. He used to keep it hanging on a timber in the heading, but he must have had it with him on the day he died because although we could hear it ticking away, we never could find it."

Jeff took a drink and continued. "After a few days, the ticking stopped, and we thought no more of it. Until the day that Amos and Joshua heard the sound of a watch ticking in their seam. They were working a small seam—about twenty-eight inches wide—lying on their sides in the mud. Suddenly, clear as day, they could hear the steady tick, tick, tick of a watch. They looked around, trying to see where the sound was coming from, puzzled because old Ted's watch had been buried on the other side of the mine. Amos started crawling out, carrying his load, and Josh followed right behind him. But suddenly the seam caved in. Killed Josh instantly. Amos was real shook up."

Jeff and Jim finished their lunch in silence and went back to work.

"Did anyone ever find the watch?" Jim asked after a few minutes.

"Nope. But people kept hearing it. The ticking sound would move through the mine, turning up first one place, then another. Wherever it was heard, there would be a fatal accident. Luke was killed in an explosion the morning after the fire boss heard a watch ticking while he was making his nightly inspection round. Robert choked to death on some bad air the day after hearing a watch ticking in his section of the mine. And there have been others."

Jim watched Jeff carefully, trying to see if his brother-in-law was pulling his leg. But Jeff was serious. Jeff was trying to warn him.

"I've never heard it myself. And I'm right glad of it," Jeff said.

Jeff wouldn't talk about the death watch after that first day, but other miners told Jim more about it. Its tick was louder than a normal watch, and no one could predict where or when the ticking sound would turn up. The miners feared the death watch more than they feared the devil. Some miners, upon hearing the ticking sound, had tried to smash the walls with their picks in an attempt to destroy the watch. One fellow tried to blow it up with a stick of dynamite. He blew himself up instead. The death watch was relentless: ticking away the seconds of some poor man's life, ignoring the curses the miners heaped upon it, inflicting itself upon all who were marked for death.

Jim was still half-convinced that the men were playing a joke on him. According to the fire boss, the death watch had not been heard ticking for many months. Jim had just about decided to laugh off the story when young Billy Wright came running up to the seam where he was working with two other miners. Billy was shaking. "I heard the death watch. Over in Caleb's shaft. Hurry!"

They dropped everything and followed Billy at a run. They were met by a terrible wave of heat and the roar of flames.

"Fire!" Billy shouted. They raced back toward the entrance of the mine, sounding the alarm. Rescue workers poured water into the mine using water hoses until the fire was contained. Caleb was the only miner killed in the fire, which had been caused by a cable line knocked down near a wooden timber.

After the fire, Jim Kelly no longer doubted the truth of the death-watch tick. But the watch went silent, and there followed several months of peace. Jim worked so hard and so diligently that the fire boss assigned him a very tricky shaft over in a far section of the mine, a compliment to Jim's skill. Then, one morning as Jim came up the gangway, the fire boss waved him aside when Jim came up for his brass check.

"Jim," said the boss, looking very grave. "I want you to go back home."

"Go back home?" Jim asked, puzzled. Had he done something wrong? "Why? What's the matter?"

"In the name of God, Jim, go back home," the fire boss repeated. "Just do as I tell you. You'll be thanking me for it later."

Jim was frightened. He couldn't afford to be fired. He and Margaret had finally saved up enough money to rent a small cottage, but money was still very tight. Jim couldn't afford to lose a day's wages. Not with seven children to feed.

"Listen, boss. I don't understand. I thought I was giving satisfaction. Why are you calling me off?" Jim asked, feeling angry now.

The fire boss's shoulders sagged as if under a heavy weight.

"If you must know," he said slowly. "I heard the death watch ticking in your section while I was making my inspection rounds last night. If you go in there today, you won't come out."

"The death watch?" Jim gasped. He felt his heart clench, and the dinner pail rattled in his hand. Slowly, he nodded to the fire boss and turned back for home.

As he hurried toward the new cottage, Jim was filled with gratitude: He had been spared the fate of so many of his fellow miners. Glancing at his watch, he realized that he could still make the eight o'clock mass if he hurried. Wanting to give thanks for his escape from death, Jim changed quickly into his Sunday clothes and raced toward the church. When he reached the railroad grade crossing, he found the gates down. Not wishing to miss the mass, Jim jumped the gates and stepped onto the tracks.

The last thing he heard was the scream of a train whistle, as the 7:55 flyer came roaring down the tracks.

6

Seeing Ghosts

I grew up on Sea Island, Georgia, where my old Granny used to tell us that there was a trick to seeing ghosts. Well, I was a young and foolish boy back in those days, and I was just plain excited to hear that common folk could experience ghosts. I demanded to know exactly how it was done.

"Gabriel," my Granny said, "if you take the wet coating from a dog's eye and stick it in yer own eye, then you can see ghosts. But don't you go trying nothing, Gabriel. They're bad news, them ghosts."

"Of course not, Granny," says I, with my most angelic smile. Oh, I was a bit of a scamp in those days. Always up to my ears in trouble.

I couldn't wait to try out my new skill. As soon as everyone was distracted after dinner, I sneaked up on my old dog, Lion. Now Lion, he liked to curl up by the fireplace at nighttime. He was snoozin' away all cozy, and he never guessed I was sneaking up on him until I stuck my finger in his eye. Well Lion, he shot near up to the ceiling with a terrible yelp and then jumped right

SEEING GHOSTS

out the window. Goodbye, dog. Lucky for Lion, we'd left the window open that night.

"Gabriel," yelled Granny from the kitchen. "What's wrong with Lion?"

"He musta heard something outside, Granny," I fibbed.

Once Granny started talking to my Ma again, I rubbed the finger I'd stuck in Lion's eye into my own eye, grabbed my cap, and left the house. I'd only traveled about a hundred feet toward the woods when a huge white mist started forming in front of my eyes. It moved like a swarm of birds, but I knew it weren't birds, 'cause each of them things had two long legs and two long arms. They started flying around like buzzards, and came right at me with a woofing sound. I let out a yelp and ducked to the ground as they flew right over me. My heart was hammering near out of my chest, and my hands were shaking. I never realized seeing ghosts could be so scary.

When I looked up again, the night was dark and there were no more bird-ghosts. I was feeling a little queasy after my narrow escape, but as I said before, I was foolish in those days, so I kept walking into the woods.

Just where the path narrows a bit, I heard a hissing sound. A strip of light started rising from a fallen log near the creek. The rope of light was squirming upward like a snake, and suddenly it opened two black eyes and I saw it was a ghost snake. It opened its mouth and a forked tongue reached for me. I let out a terrified squeak, closed my eyes, and ran for my life. I seemed to hear that snake slithering behind me as I bumped into tree branches, tripped over some roots, and finally banged square into a broad tree trunk. I kept pumping my arms for a while, but I finally realized I wasn't getting anywhere with that tree in the way. So I stopped running. I didn't want to open my eyes, but since I had no idea where I was, I decided to chance it. I opened my eyes just a wee bit, but all I could see was the bark of the tree nearly touching my eyelashes. I pushed away from the tree and looked around for the snake, but it was gone.

I made my way back to the path, keeping my eyes on the ground 'cause I didn't want to see any more ghosts. There was a rustling sound to my right, and I shut my eyes real quick and started running again. I could hear that ghost running with me, and then it must have gotten in front of me, 'cause I tripped and tumbled head over heels. I kept my eyes shut even though I could feel the breath of that ghost on my face, and it kept licking me. Then I realized it was Lion.

Feeling foolish, I opened up my eyes and said, "Stupid dog." I grabbed him and gave him a hug and sat up. Then I saw the most terrifying sight of all. A lady, all in white, was rising slowly from what looked like an open grave. She moaned as she stepped out of the ground, and she pointed her finger right at us. Me and Lion, we moaned too, and we took to our heels and ran as fast as we could for home. We didn't even wait to open the front door, we just threw ourselves in the same window that Lion had jumped out of and dived under the hearth rug.

We stayed under that rug until Ma came into the parlor to send me up to bed. Granny came with her, and when she saw me under the rug she just laughed and laughed. She knew what I had done. She told me to make sure I cleaned my eye out with water before I went to sleep, 'cause who knew what ghosts might be haunting this house. I shot right out to the kitchen and got some water from the bucket to clean my eye with. And I never took the coat out of a dog's eye again. Once was plenty for me.

7

The Headless Haunt

The evening was windy and cold. It was a bad night to be out walking, but the old man and his wife kept pushing their way through the thick mud on the road, trying to reach their son's house. Darkness had fallen swiftly, and threatening clouds hovered overhead.

"Mother, I reckon my feet are nigh on frozen," the old man said after a while. "And I'm hungry enough to eat a horse."

"Well, Father, I think we should find a place to stay the night," his wife replied, hugging her shawl tightly around her. "I reckon Junior won't mind if we don't arrive till morning."

Heartened by this decision, the old couple kept watch for a place to spend the night. Soon they saw a house through the thick trees that lined the muddy road. As they approached, they saw that it was quite a grand house, with smoke rising from the chimney and firelight flickering in many windows.

"Father, I reckon the folks who live here are rich," the old woman said to her husband. "We'd best go around to the back door."

"Whatever you think best," said the old man, who didn't care which door they used, as long as they got in out of the cold.

THE HEADLESS HAUNT

They went around to the back porch and knocked on the door. A man's voice called, "Come in." So in they went.

They found themselves in a large kitchen with a fire in the hearth and skillets waiting as if someone was about to prepare supper. But there was no one in the room. They looked around, but they didn't see the man who bade them enter. The old woman saw a rabbit boiling in a covered pot, and she smelled beans baking. On the wide wooden table were meat and flour and lard.

"Somebody's cooking dinner," the old woman told her husband, who was warming his hands over the fire. "I wonder where they be?"

"Seems a bit strange, them running off just after they told us to come in," said the old man. "But meanwhile, Mother, take off your wet shoes and stockings and get yourself warmed up. I'll run out and fill up those buckets at the springhouse we passed so we can have some coffee. Maybe our host will make himself known while I'm outside."

"I'll get the brown beans and that molly cottontail and that cornbread ready for our dinner in three shakes of a lamb's tail," the old woman said with relish as she took off her wet shoes and stockings.

The old man went out with a bucket, and the old woman sat down by the fire to toast her feet. She was just thinking about getting up and mixing up some cornbread when right through the shut door came a man with no head. The old woman gasped in fear and astonishment. The man was wearing britches, a vest, shirt, coat, and shoes. He even wore a fancy collar. But rising above it was a bloody stump where his head should have been.

"What in the name of the Lord do you want?" the old woman gasped.

And the man started to talk to her without any mouth. The words seemed to form themselves in the old woman's head as he told her how he came to be this way.

"I am in misery, madam," the man said. "I was killed by a robber who was after my money. He removed my head with a cutlass and then took me to the cellar and buried my head on one side and my body on the other. Then this villain and his companions dug all around my cellar, but fortunately they did not find my treasure. Alas, they went away and left me in two pieces, doomed to haunt this house until someone should restore my head and bury me in one grave."

The old woman was moved by the ghost's story. "How is it no one has ever restored you?" she asked.

"There have been others, madam, who have entered this house. But as none addressed me in the name of the Lord, I was unable to speak to them."

At that moment the door swung open, passing right through the body of the ghost. The old man hurried in with his bucket full of water, stamping his feet to get the mud off.

"Mother, it's plumb cold out there," he said, setting the bucket on the shelf. He turned back toward the door, intending to shut it, and saw the ghost. The old man gasped and backed away, his horrified gaze on the bloody stump where the ghost's head should be.

"It's all right, Father," the old woman said hastily, closing the door against the cold. "Sir, please tell my husband your tale, in the name of the Lord."

So the ghost told the old man his story. When the ghost finished, he asked the old couple to go to the cellar and find his head so he could be buried in one grave.

"If, in your kindness, you restore me, I will show you where my treasure is buried," the headless haunt concluded.

The old man looked at his wife, who nodded. "We will surely help you," he told the ghost. "Just let me get a torch and a shovel."

"You will not need a torch," said the ghost. With great dignity, he walked to the fire and stuck his finger in it. The finger blazed up as bright as any torch. He pointed to the place where the shovels were kept and then led the old couple down into the dark cellar by the light of his finger.

"There. That is where my head is buried," said the ghost, pointing toward the north end of the cellar, "and there is where my body is buried," he finished, pointing toward a hole in the south corner. "But dig here first, and you will find my barrels of silver and gold."

The headless haunt lit up a section of the floor, and the old couple started to dig. They dug until the old woman was almost worn out. They were deep under the cellar floor. Then the old man's shovel made a hollow thump as he pushed it into the soil, and they soon uncovered several barrels filled with gold and silver. The old woman sat on her heels, running her fingers through the beautiful coins, lit by the blazing finger of the ghost. With tears in her eyes, she said, "Oh, thank you, sir. Thank you. And now, we must restore your head to you."

Her husband, who was staring speechlessly at the gold and silver, came out of his trance and said, "That we must, Mother. Good sir, if you will show us again where your head is buried?"

The old man helped his wife out of the pit and they followed the ghost to the corner where his head was buried. A few turns of the shovel produced the head, and the husband lifted it with the shovel and offered it to the ghost. The haunt reached over with dignity, took his head in his hands, and put it on his neck. Then he lit several candles with his burning finger so the old couple would have light to remove the gold and silver from the pit they had dug. He blew out his finger, and, still keeping a firm grip on his head, walked over to the south corner and sank through the floor into the place where his body was buried. Just before his head sank into the ground, he said, "Thank you, good sir and kind madam."

As soon as the last bit of the ghost disappeared, the ground shook and the house trembled above their heads. Then a voice came from under the ground: "You have restored me! I am now buried together, head and corpse. Because of your kindness, I give you my land, my house, and my money. May you be as rich as I was and come to a more honorable end."

The old man and his wife stared at one another in shock for a moment. Then the old woman smiled and picked up one of the candles the headless haunt had lit for them.

"Come Father," she said. "We have the rest of our lives to count this gold. But that cottontail will be boiled over if we wait much longer to eat supper."

The old man took the other candle and helped his wife up the stairs. They were covered with dirt from their digging, so they washed themselves clean with lye soap. Then the old woman mixed up a batch of cornbread and the old man made some coffee with the water from the springhouse, and they had a wonderful supper of cottontail and cornbread and brown beans and hot coffee.

And the old man and the old woman lived in the grand house for the rest of their days, with money to spare for food and clothing. When they died at last of old age, they left a large inheritance for their grandchildren. And no one ever saw the headless haunt again.

8

The Baseball Game

BIRMINGHAM, ALABAMA

As soon as Uncle Henry heard about the big barbecue and baseball game in the next town, he was absolutely determined to go. Uncle Henry once pitched for the local team, and he still loved to see a good ball game. So he got up early on Saturday morning and took the train down to the game.

Uncle Henry looked around until he found himself a good seat on one of the wagons lining the far end of the pasture where the barbecue and ball game were to take place. Pretty soon, the ballplayers came riding up on their big horses and crowded around the barbecue to get some food. There were a lot of people, and Uncle Henry had to fight his way through the laughing, arguing throng to get something to eat. The ballplayers had to rest for a bit under the big tree at the side of the field after eating too much barbecue. Then, as the spectators settled down with their food, the ballplayers started warming up on the field.

Uncle Henry reclaimed his spot on the wagon and ate with a good appetite. This was going to be a humdinger of a game, judging from the antics going on during the warm-up session. It was getting late, and Uncle Henry grew impatient. Why wasn't

THE BASEBALL GAME

the game starting? He asked a fellow what was happening and was told that one of the pitchers lived quite a ways out of town and hadn't arrived. A few minutes later, the pitcher rode up on his horse and ran out onto the field to warm up.

By the time the game started, it was late in the afternoon. Uncle Henry knew that he was going to miss the train back home if he stayed for the whole game, but it was so exciting that he just didn't care. He would walk home along the tracks.

What Uncle Henry hadn't planned on was the game going until it was nearly too dark to see. But what a game! It was tied right up until the very end, and then an unexpected home run decided the game in the home team's favor. Uncle Henry yelled himself hoarse with excitement.

And then it was over, and Uncle Henry realized he had to walk home in the dark. Uncle Henry never minded the long walk in the daytime, but walking the railroad tracks at night was not something he looked forward to. And how in tarnation was he going to see? At that moment, Uncle Henry spied a bottle on the ground beside the wagon, and he got an idea. He stopped at the local grocery store and bought enough kerosene to fill the bottle. Then he took off his necktie, folded it, and stuffed it into the bottle of kerosene like a wick. As soon as the tie was lit, Uncle Henry started walking down the railroad tracks toward home, using the bottle as a lantern to light his way.

The night got darker and darker. Storm clouds covered the sky, and Uncle Henry was getting mighty scared. He kept imagining that eyes were peering at him from beside the railroad tracks. Finally, Uncle Henry lost his nerve and started running as fast as his legs could carry him. Suddenly, a huge white dog with red eyes appeared, standing in the center of the tracks.

Uncle Henry stopped dead and stared at the dog. It seemed to grow larger and larger the longer he looked at it in the light from his bottle.

"Get back!" Uncle Henry shouted, waving the bottle at the dog. The necktie slipped out of the bottle and the light extinguished on the ground as the dog backed off a pace, its red eyes still glowing at Uncle Henry. Uncle Henry knew he was a goner. He ran for his life past the big white dog, hoping to get home before it could catch him. The big white dog ran after him, right on his heels, panting. Luckily, the dog's wild red eyes seemed to light the track so Uncle Henry did not stumble as he ran. Uncle Henry veered off the tracks when he got near home and ran through his neighbors' yards until he reached his own house. He didn't hear the dog chasing him anymore, and he collapsed on the front porch to try to catch his breath.

Aunt Jenny heard him fall onto the porch and came out with the lantern from the kitchen. When she saw him lying on the floorboards, she ran inside and brought him a dipper of well water. Uncle Henry drank it in one gulp and sat up. He drank two more dippers before he was ready to tell Aunt Jenny about the white dog chasing him all the way home.

When he finished his story, Aunt Jenny shook her head. "Uncle Henry, you're the strangest fellow I ever knew," she laughed at him. "That weren't an evil spirit, that was one of your friends come back from the grave to escort you home safely 'cause you stayed too long at that ball game."

Uncle Henry shook his head stubbornly. "Only reason I'm here is that I ran faster than that dog," he said.

He let Aunt Jenny pull him up, and she sat him down to a nice supper of collard greens, meat, and cracklin' bread.

The next morning, their next-door neighbor Jonathan stopped by to tell Uncle Henry and Aunt Jenny the latest news. The sheriff had caught two robbers lurking near the railroad tracks after the ball game.

"According to the sheriff," Jonathan said, "he's been trying to catch those thieves for a long while. They're always lurking near the tracks on ball game nights, waiting to rob people walking home from games. Sheriff says they're the ones that killed that fellow after the game last month. Lucky for everyone, the robbers were scared off by a big white dog near the train station last night, and the sheriff caught 'em."

"A white dog, did you say?" asked Aunt Jenny, glancing over at Uncle Henry, who had turned pale when he heard Jonathan's news.

"Yep. They were real scared of it. Told the sheriff it had red, glowing eyes and grew larger every time they looked at it. Guess the sheriff must have hit 'em too hard on the head," Jonathan said with a grin. "Well, I'd best pass the news along to the Smiths."

He hurried out the door on his way to the Smith house across the road. Aunt Jenny looked over at Uncle Henry as she closed the door behind him.

"You still think that white dog was an evil spirit?" she asked.

"No," Uncle Henry said, sitting down shakily on a chair.

"I think that white dog saved your life," Aunt Jenny said, sitting down opposite him. Uncle Henry nodded, speechless for once in his life.

"And you know what else I think?" asked Aunt Jenny. "I think you'd best get home before dark from now on."

"I think you're right," said Uncle Henry.

9

Chattanooga's Ghost

NEW ORLEANS, LOUISIANA

My pal Chattanooga was just about the best roustabout that ever worked a steamboat here in New Orleans. But he had one vice, as the preacher would say. Some roustabouts drank their pay away, but not Chattanooga. Chattanooga smoked his pay away. As soon as we were paid, Chattanooga'd go down to the store and spend his pay on expensive cigars. It was a terrible shame. Chattanooga's clothes were always in tatters, and some weeks he'd have to catch fish to eat 'cause he'd spent all his money on cigars. Worst thing about it, to my mind, was the fact that he wouldn't let me smoke even one of those cigars. And I was his best friend.

"Piece o' Man," he'd say to me, "I love ya like a brother. But if ya want a cigar, ya gotta go buy it for yourself."

"Chattanooga," I'd say back to him, "if you worked harder and smoked less, you'd have more money. I've got money 'cause I don't smoke."

Chattanooga would just laugh and walk over to the icehouse to get a cigar. That's where he kept them, in the icehouse. Chattanooga claimed that keeping them in the icehouse made cigars taste right. I didn't notice any difference myself the day

43

CHATTANOOGA'S GHOST

I snuck one of his cigars out of the icehouse. It tasted just the same as all the other ones I'd ever bought. But Chattanooga was an expert smoker, so I guess he knew what he was talking about.

Every night after supper, Chattanooga would go get one of his expensive cigars out of the icehouse, sit down in his favorite chair, and start smoking. I usually sat with him, and we'd gossip and tell jokes. While we were talking, Chattanooga would blow one, two, three smoke rings. He tried to make them as big as he could. When three of the rings would line up in front of him, he'd light a match and throw it through all three smoke rings at once. It was a great trick. Chattanooga said he'd seen it in a show once and practiced it till he got it just right. Word got around the docks, just like it always did, and many a night we'd have two or three roustabouts stop by to see Chattanooga's trick.

One night, Chattanooga was working late hauling coal off a fuel flat. He must have tripped while he was wheeling his load, 'cause he fell into the river and was drowned before anyone could get to him. Oh my, I was laid down with sorrow. My best friend was gone, and I wouldn't ever see him again.

The next night after supper, I went and sat in my chair near the icehouse. Chattanooga's chair stood empty beside mine, and I was feeling mighty low. Chattanooga had left almost a month's supply of cigars in the icehouse, but I didn't feel like smoking any.

Just then, the door of the icehouse opened. I looked around and saw Chattanooga standing inside the icehouse, picking up cigars and feeling them over, like he always did, trying to get the best one. I jumped to my feet.

"Chattanooga," I shouted. "I thought you were dead!"

I stepped toward the icehouse and then stopped suddenly, realizing I could see right through Chattanooga's body. For a moment, I was chilled to the bone. He was a ghost. But as I watched Chattanooga carefully picking out a cigar, I just couldn't stay scared. He might be a ghost, but he was still my pal Chattanooga.

He ignored me completely, carefully putting all the cigars back into the box except the one he thought was the best. Then he walked right out the icehouse door. I stepped aside quick, 'cause I didn't want any ghost—not even Chattanooga's—walking through me.

Chattanooga sat down in his chair, lit up the cigar, and began smoking. He didn't seem to see me, and didn't answer me when I called his name. Still, it was a comfort to see him enjoying his cigar. I sat down next to him and watched him blowing smoke rings. One, two, three large smoke rings floated up in the air. Chattanooga lit a match and tossed it at the smoke rings. It went through the first ring, but fell short of the second. Chattanooga's ghost frowned. He blew three more smoke rings, and tried again. The second time, the match made it through the first two rings, but not the third.

"Bad luck, Chattanooga," I said.

Chattanooga's ghost didn't answer. He just went on smoking and blowing smoke rings and trying to throw a lighted match through all three rings at once. Chattanooga finished his cigar before he managed to do his trick, and he cussed something awful before he disappeared into thin air.

I wasn't surprised the next night when I met Chattanooga's ghost coming out of the icehouse with a cigar. I sat beside him and told him about my day, even though he didn't seem to hear me. He just blew smoke rings and tried to throw the lighted match through them. He kept burning his fingers and cussing because no matter how many times he tried, Chattanooga couldn't get the match through all three smoke rings. Finally he ground out the cigar, cussed once more, and disappeared. Boy, was he mad. I had never seen Chattanooga madder than that.

For about a month, Chattanooga would join me each night after supper. He would smoke and blow smoke rings and burn match after match trying to do his trick. He never got it right. I guess death does that to you. But Chattanooga kept trying. Each night, he would get madder and madder, and one night Chattanooga up and disappeared right out of his chair with a loud popping noise. He hadn't even finished his cigar.

The next evening, Chattanooga appeared as usual in the icehouse. I waited for him to choose his cigar and come out to sit with me, but he just stood in the icehouse looking at something. Finally, I went in to see what was keeping him. I looked where he was looking and saw that Chattanooga's cigar box was empty. Chattanooga had smoked all his cigars. My heart dropped into my toes. I turned to look at Chattanooga and saw that he was holding one last cigar in his hand. He shook his head sadly, nodding at the empty box.

Then, for the first and last time, Chattanooga's ghost spoke to me: "This one's for you, Piece o' Man. Have a cigar."

Chattanooga handed me his last cigar, and then he disappeared. I knew it was the last time I would ever see him.

I went out and sat in my seat and smoked that cigar as slow as I could. When I was down to the last little bit, I blew smoke rings, one, two, three. Then I lit a match and threw it at those smoke rings. The match went right through all three rings, like it used to when Chattanooga was alive. Just for a moment, I could see the dim outline of Chattanooga's ghost sitting in his chair. He laughed and said, "Good one, Piece o' Man."

Then I was alone again.

10

Hold Him, Tabb

"I remember what it was like before the railroad came through these parts," Uncle Jeter reminisced, tapping the stem of his pipe against his cheek as he relaxed into the most comfortable chair by the fire.

I was sitting on a stool right next to the fireplace, occasionally throwing on another log, impatient for him to continue. Uncle Jeter told the best stories about the old days, but he wouldn't be rushed. I knew from previous experience that if I tried to hurry him, he would clam up and refuse to tell any stories at all. So I just waited, trying not to fidget.

"Back in those days, Matthew my boy, men had to be tough. I used to earn my living by carting supplies from town to town on horse-drawn wagons. Not easy work, no sir. Especially in winter."

Uncle Jeter paused to light his pipe with a small stick he took from the fireplace.

"One cold December day," he continued after the pipe was lit to his satisfaction, "I was traveling together with a number of wagons. About the middle of the afternoon, it began to snow. We decided mighty quick that we should stop somewhere and

49

Hold Him, Tabb

wait until morning to continue on. Old Ned, the tinsmith, he was the one who spotted an abandoned settlement near the roadside. It looked like a good place to ride out the storm. There was an old house and a barn with plenty of stalls for all our horses."

Uncle Jeter paused for a moment and shook his head. "We thought we were real lucky, finding such a good shelter. We were just about through unhitching the horses from the wagons when a fellow stopped by to talk to us. Claimed he was the owner of the property. Told us we were welcome to stay but the house was haunted. 'Haunted?' Tabb, a tinker traveling with us, asked. 'What do you mean, haunted?' The owner said that no one who had ever stayed in that house had made it out alive, not for the last twenty-five years. That was good enough for me. I hitched Ol' Betsy back up to the wagon and moved up the road about half a mile to where a stand of trees offered some shelter from the snow. Everyone else followed me, except for Tabb. He thought we were plumb foolish, and said so. He wasn't afraid of no ghosts, and he didn't plan on perishing in the snow with the rest of us.

"I was real uneasy about that, but I wasn't about to risk my neck in a haunted house. I stayed next to the road, though. I could see that Tabb had settled into the house nice and comfy, 'cause there was a light in the window and I saw smoke coming from the chimney. The rest of us built a fire as best we could and huddled together for warmth through the long night. I wondered a couple of times if Tabb wasn't the smart one and we the foolish. But the owner of the settlement had looked like an honest fellow, and he seemed right scared of that house, so I figured there must be something to it."

Uncle Jeter was so involved in his story now that he let his pipe go out.

"So what happened?" I asked.

"Well, just about dawn, I gave up trying to sleep and went back down the road to see how Tabb had fared for the night. I didn't go into the house, but I did peek through the windows on the first floor. When I got round the back, I saw Tabb snoozing peacefully in a big bed. He looked warm and happy. Then I saw a movement on the ceiling. I looked up, and there was a large man dressed all in white, floating flat against the ceiling. The man was right over Tabb, looking down on him. Scared me out of my wits.

" 'Tabb,' I hissed, tapping at the window. 'Tabb, get out of there you fool!'

"Tabb woke up at once, but instead of looking toward the window, he looked straight up and saw the man in white on the ceiling. Tabb gave an awful yell, but before he could move out of bed that man fell down off the ceiling and landed right on top of him. Now Tabb was a big, strong fellow, but that ghost was powerful, and Tabb couldn't get the ghost to let him go. They wrestled back and forth on the bed. Sometimes Tabb would be on top and sometimes the ghost. I gave a shout and smashed the glass in the window, shouting 'Hold him, Tabb, hold him!'

" 'You can bet yer soul I've got him,' Tabb panted as he and the ghost fell off the bed.

"I could hear shouts behind me as I started to crawl in the window. The other wagoneers had heard the commotion and came to see what was wrong. Just then, the ghost flung himself and Tabb right at me, knocking me back out of the window and into the snow. The ghost levitated himself and Tabb right up onto the roof of the front porch. We all ran around the house to get a better view, shouting, 'Hold him, Tabb. Hold him!' The ghost and Tabb were wrestling frantically in the snow on the porch roof.

" 'You can bet yer life I've got him,' gasped Tabb.

"The ghost gave a mighty leap and threw Tabb onto the roof of the house.

" 'Hold him Tabb,' I shouted with the other men. 'Hold him!'

" 'You can bet yer boots I've got him,' Tabb yelled as he and the ghost tumbled over and over on the roof. Snow was pouring off the roof on all sides as they struggled. And then the ghost lifted Tabb right into the air.

" 'Hold him Tabb,' old Ned shouted. 'Hold him.' The rest of us were silent.

" 'I got him,' Tabb cried. 'But he got me too!'

"They were floating a few feet off the roof, still grappling with each other. And then the ghost carried Tabb straight up into the air. We watched them until they were both out of sight."

Uncle Jeter slowly leaned back into his chair.

"What happened to Tabb?" I cried. Uncle Jeter shook his head.

"None of us ever saw Tabb again," he said.

11

Steal Away Home

I knew Thursday was the day to run—yes, sweet Lawd—when I heard my auntie singing in the harvest field: "Swing low, sweet chariot, coming for to carry me home." That was Moses's song, and I knew it meant that she'd received word that Moses—Harriet Tubman—had made another trip south. If I hurried, I could maybe jump on the Glory Train with Moses and ride "home" to Canada!

My mammy and my pappy had both run north when I was little, and my mammy's sister had looked after me 'til I grew big and strong. My aunt's man had a bad leg and would never be able to run, and she refused to leave him. But she always kept track of the railroad signals, and she'd been teaching me everything she'd ever heard about the way north.

My auntie had a rich, wonderful voice, and she always sang when she worked in the fields. She used the songs to teach me how to escape. "Follow the Drinking Gourd" was the song she used to show me the group of stars that told a-body where the North Star was. "Wade in the Water" taught me to stay near water and jump into it if I heard bloodhounds baying. And whenever she had something new to tell me, she'd sing "Steal

STEAL AWAY HOME

Away Home," and that meant I was to meet her in the woods to talk about the Glory Train.

Sure enough, as soon as my auntie was done singing about the chariot, she started singing "Steal Away Home." Yes, Lawd, today was the day! I met my auntie in the woods after sunset. She'd put together a little bag with my best Sunday clothes to wear when I got to town so I wouldn't look like a runaway slave, and some food. She wrapped me up good in my uncle's jacket, 'cause the winter nights were cold, and she told me to look for a house with a lantern on a hitching post or a Jacob's Ladder quilt hung on the railing; both signs that the place was a "depot" where I could sleep safe for the night and maybe get a good meal.

I kissed my auntie and promised to buy her and my uncle's freedom when I was a rich man living in Canada. Then I ran as softly and as swiftly as I knew how. Moses was meeting a group about two days' north of here, and I had to get there by Saturday, which was always the day that Moses took her passengers north—or risk missing the Glory Train.

I knew the first few miles well, but soon I was in new territory, making my way through swampy land and avoiding the road. My auntie told me it was best to sleep and eat off the land until I reached my conductor. It was cold—yes, Lawd—the coldest winter I could remember, but I kept myself wrapped up good and ate only a little bread at a time. I even found some roots to chew on. It was enough to keep me alive, but it weren't tasty and it didn't keep the rumble out of my belly.

To keep my mind off my hunger, I thought about Moses. Harriet Tubman had been born a slave, just like me, right here in Maryland. She worked as a house servant when she was little and then went out into the fields as soon as she grew big and strong. When she was a teenager, she was hurt in the head trying to protect another slave from an angry overseer, who threw a two-pound weight that hit Harriet instead of the other slave. All the rest of her life, Moses suffered from that head injury, sometimes falling into a heavy sleep right out of the blue.

She later ran away from her master because she was afraid she was going to be sold, following the North Star each night until she reached Philadelphia. Since Pennsylvania was a free state, she settled there and got a job. After about a year, she decided to join the Underground Railroad and help other slaves find their way north. She rescued her sister and her sister's children, her brother, and many others.

I paused to eat a little more of the bread around dusk the next day, and that's when I heard the bloodhounds baying. I hadn't planned on pursuit, at least not right away, but apparently my master had already spread the news that I was missing. I tossed my bread back into my sack and I ran—oh yes, Lawd—I ran as fast as my legs would go, until I found me a stream. I waded until I thought my feet would freeze off, and then climbed from tree to tree like a squirrel before dropping back into the stream to wade some more. I didn't hear them dogs again, but I was so chilled that I knew I needed shelter or I'd die of the cold.

I took a risk and went out onto the road for awhile, hoping to find a depot. I couldn't believe my eyes when the first house I saw through the growing darkness had a lantern on the hitching post. I turned into the lane, shivering something fierce, and realized that the house was dark. No one was home. What was I going to do? Them dogs were still out there, and I had to find shelter or at least build me a fire.

As I stood there, too cold and numb to think, I saw a pretty golden-haired lady wearing a long white dress come around the corner of the house. She held a lantern in her hand that lit up her figure until it glowed. I thought she must be an angel. She beckoned to me, and I followed her at once, not doubting for a minute that she would help me. She led me through the yard to an old woodpile. Leaning over it, she pointed to some logs piled in the corner and motioned for me to move them.

The lady held the lantern for me to see while I shifted the logs and found a trapdoor underneath them. I pulled the heavy door open and looked down into a dark pit. The woman lowered the lantern into the darkness, and I saw a ladder and some blankets and in the corner, a canteen of water. I scampered down the ladder right quick, calling my thanks, and heard the trapdoor close above me. Several thumps told me that the lady was piling logs back on top of the door to keep it hidden. In the darkness, I pulled a stub of candle from my sack—the Lawd bless and keep my auntie—and lit it with a match. I drank the canteen dry and curled up among the blankets.

I woke up once, some time later, hearing the sound of baying bloodhounds, but they didn't come near the secret root cellar under the woodpile, and I went back to sleep. The next time I woke, it was because the trapdoor was being pulled open. A young farmer's face appeared in the square of light above me. When he saw me, his eyes widened in shock. He stared at me as if I were a ghost. Finally, after a few ragged breaths, the farmer said: "Son, how did you get in here?"

I was puzzled. Hadn't the pretty lady told her husband I was here? I explained at once about running away, and about the bloodhounds and the pretty lady in white who hid me. Another look of shock flickered over the man's face when I mentioned the woman.

"What's the matter?" I asked apprehensively. The man shook his head and told me it was safe to come in the house.

He hid me in an upstairs room and brought me some hot food. Then he sat in a chair beside me and showed me a small painting of a pretty golden-haired lady wearing a long, white dress. It was the woman who had hidden me.

"My wife," the young man said, tears springing to his eyes. "She died six months ago."

I thought I would die myself, right on the spot, as his words sank into my head. I had been hidden by a ghost! Great Lawd in heaven! A ghost!

"She was the only other person alive who knew about that root cellar," the young man said at last. "I saw her in a dream last night, and she told me that she'd put something in there for me. That was the reason I opened the trapdoor this morning, because of seeing her face in my dream. I hadn't been down there for a good six months before then."

I must have looked as shook up as he was, 'cause the farmer gave me a sip of brandy to steady my nerves and told me to get some sleep. He told me he would hide me under the false seat in his wagon and take me to another safe house after dark. Which was just what he did.

I never did meet up with Moses, but I did make it first to Philadelphia, then up to Rochester, and finally to freedom in Canada. Yes, Lawd! It was hard traveling all by myself. It took me a long time—eighty-nine days—and I got plenty tired of swamps and riverbanks and having nothing to eat but roots and leaves. But at last I was free! I found my parents living in Ontario, and we saved up enough to buy freedom for my auntie and uncle and bring them to Canada too. Hallelujah!

60

The Waves Call

GREENVILLE, MISSISSIPPI

The Mississippi River is seething with ghosts of all kinds. Doesn't matter where you visit on the riverfront, you're going to find ghosts. There are tales of murdered seamen, river pirates, roustabouts, wharf rats, and even a few old explorers who haunt the shores of the mighty river. But one ghost wasn't there to scare anybody. He was there to try to save someone: a roustabout named Jakie Walker.

Now Jakie had been working the wharves for nigh on thirty years, and he knew the river pretty well—her secrets, her tricks, and her moods. Jakie was a good roustabout and a fine man. But his one vice was drinking, and it caused a lot of stress on his marriage. Jakie's wife was a strong-minded woman who didn't put much store in drinking. She would harp and yell and beat on Jakie whenever he came home drunk. It wasn't a pretty thing.

Well, one night Jakie went out drinking with his buddies and got himself quite liquored up. It was very late when the party ended, and his friends all headed for home. But Jakie didn't want to go home just yet. He was worried about what his wife was going to say when he came home drunk again, so he decided to wait until he sobered up a bit before going

THE WAVES CALL

home. He walked about for a while, finally drifting down to the wharves where he worked.

Jakie sat down on the edge of the docks and listened to the water lapping the shore. It was very quiet and dark by the riverside. A soft breeze was blowing on Jakie's face. He gazed across the whispering river, feeling at peace with the world. There was a dark place right out in the center that Jakie did not remember seeing before. As he studied the spot in the dim light, it grew darker and began to swirl. The breeze turned cold, and Jakie shivered.

Before his eyes, the darkness took the shape of a man wearing a long black gown that seemed to drag behind the figure into an unfathomable distance. The breeze grew stronger and colder. Jakie sat frozen in place, unable to take his eyes off the figure as it slowly began to glide toward him on top of the water. Jakie wanted to scream, to holler, to run away, but he couldn't move.

As the figure drew near, Jakie felt an incredible heat burning like a bolt of lightning through the cold breeze. He felt as if his cold body had suddenly caught on fire. The black eyes of the man pierced deep into his soul as if the man was trying to crawl into Jakie's mind. For a terrible moment, Jakie was sure that the figure was going to drag him down to hell.

Fear loosened Jakie's tongue, as the hot breath of the ghost blew onto his face. "What do you want, ghost? What do you want?" Jakie yelled. He tried to crawl away from the figure, but his arms and legs wouldn't move. It felt as if invisible ropes were tying him to the spot.

For a long, long moment, there was silence, except for the whisper of the river. Jakie stared in horror at the ghost. The ghost stared right back at Jakie. Then the ghost opened its arms wide, like a figure on a cross. Jakie thought that the ghost was going to grab him and that he would be buried in the long black robe that stretched into eternity. Jakie moaned in terror. "Don't touch me," he whimpered. "I ain't got nothin' you want. Nothin' at all."

The ghost spoke then in a deep, hellish voice. "The waves call me," it wailed. "They call me and I must return to them. But I will not move a step from here until I speak to you, Jakie."

Jakie swallowed. "What you want to speak to me for?" he asked.

"You knew me, Jakie, when I was alive. You knew me, but I will not tell you who I was. My name does not matter. I was drowned in the Mississippi River and now I am a ghost, haunting the waters and banks I once knew."

Jakie frantically tried to remember all the men he knew who had drowned in the Mississippi. If he could figure out the name of this ghost, maybe he could send it away. But there were too many names, from roustabouts to river captains. Jakie could not remember them all.

The ghost continued. "I have something to tell you, Jakie. You are doomed to leave this earth soon, just as I did, unless you stop your drinking."

Jakie was taken aback. He stared at the ghost incredulously. In spite of his terror, Jakie was insulted. This ghost had some nerve coming to him in the middle of the night and trying to rectify his drinking. Didn't he get enough of that from his wife and the preacher?

As if he could read Jakie's mind, the ghost said, "I was sent to take you away with me. You are doomed to share my watery grave. The waves are calling for you, as they call to me. But you are a good man, Jakie, aside from your drinking. If you promise to stop drinking, you can avoid my fate. Tell me now, boy. What is your determination in this matter?"

Jakie was really indignant now. But he still felt stuck and unable to move, so he had to stay and answer the ghost. Jakie thought about the ghost's threat to drown him. Then he contemplated life without liquor. Jakie didn't have to think long.

"Ghost," Jakie said. "Drinkin' is the chief pleasure of my life. I ain't stoppin' for no one."

The ghost studied him closely. Jakie shuddered a bit. The burning feeling was back, and Jakie was terrified all over again. But Jakie didn't care. He would not give up drinking just because some ghost showed up to scare him.

"Jakie," the ghost said in a terrible, deep voice. "I cannot accept that answer."

Jakie thought fast. He didn't want to drown. And this ghost seemed awfully serious. If only he could figure out its name. Slyly he asked, "Do you know my wife?"

"I do," the ghost said ponderously. "And I can understand why you drink. But if you do not promise me you will stop, I must take you with me under the waves."

Jakie frowned mulishly at the ghost. He ran the names of several drowned roustabouts through his mind. But the ghost spoke like it had book learning, and none of the roustabouts on his list could talk as fancy as this ghost. One of the captains, perhaps? Or a townsman who drowned while out fishing? It must be someone who had lived nearby, since the ghost claimed to know his wife.

"Jakie," said the ghost. "I think you do not believe me. I think I must show you what fate has in store for you if you continue your drinking."

As the ghost spoke, it opened its arms again and the waves in the river began to rise. The wind turned into a howling nightmare, swirling around and around until it formed a funnel reaching endlessly up into the cloudy sky. The waves started shrieking like they were demons from hell. They rose higher and higher, swirling under the deadly funnel and reaching out toward Jakie like arms. The waves were calling to Jakie, beckoning him into the depths of the Mississippi River. Jakie shouted out name after name of the men he knew who had drowned, but those waves kept coming for him, and the ghost just opened its arms wider and wider.

Jakie was defeated and he knew it. He didn't want to die. "I promise you, ghost!" he shouted over the deafening roar of the funnel and the demon-shrieking waves. "I promise you not to drink ever again. Just take away that funnel and them waves."

Immediately, the funnel and waves disappeared. The river resumed its normal course, and the night became silent and still. The ghost nodded to Jakie and glided back to the center of the river. It sank slowly under the water, and Jakie felt the invisible ropes loosen. Gingerly, Jakie pulled himself up off the dock. He was shaking with terror.

Jakie, completely sobered by his experience, ran home. He was so fearful that the ghost would change its mind and come back that he forgot to be scared of his wife. She was waiting for him by the front door. As Jakie stumbled into the front hall, his wife threw her arms around his neck.

"Jakie," she screamed. "Jakie, honey I dreamed you was dead. Jakie, I am awful glad to see you."

"Baby," Jakie gasped, hugging her back. "I almost was dead. But I'm a new man now."

Jakie never took another drink of liquor. Instead, he toted his paycheck home every week and spent each evening at home. To his surprise, the troubles with his wife just about disappeared, and Jakie became a happy family man.

13

Blackbeard's Ghost

OCRACOKE INLET, NORTH CAROLINA

"Wind's blowing inland tonight," Jeff observed casually at the dinner table that evening. Immediately, we all looked at our grandfather. He was sitting calmly at the head of the table, eating his mashed potatoes with a spoon, and ignoring us grandkids.

"No," Grandma said from her seat at the other end of the table, answering Jeff's unspoken question. "You are not going to Teach's Hole tonight. There's a storm coming and you'll be swept away and drowned, the lot of you. Then what will I tell your parents when they get home from vacation?"

"I want to see Teach's light!" shouted my twin brother, Bobby.

I wanted to see the ghost too. A local fisherman had told me about it when we went down to the docks that morning.

"Don't you want to see Teach's light, Becky?" Bobby appealed to me from across the table.

"Of course I do." We both simultaneously turned toward Grandma and said, "Please!" After ten years of being twins, we could read each other perfectly.

Grandpa was shaking his head.

BLACKBEARD'S GHOST

"Not tonight, kids. Your Grandma's right. There's a storm coming. I will take you down to Teach's Hole another night."

Bobby and Jeff, our older brother, looked as stricken as I felt. But as we continued eating, we could hear thunder coming closer, and the wind picked up and beat against the house.

"I'll tell you what," said Grandpa. "Why don't we light a fire in the fireplace and tell ghost stories? Your grandmother will make popcorn for us."

I perked up immediately. Ghost stories were perfect for a stormy night. We quickly began clearing the table as Grandma made the popcorn.

"Can we shut off all the lights?" I asked.

"Sure can," Grandpa said.

"Probably won't need to," said Grandma. "The power usually goes out."

The lights flickered a few times as she spoke. "See what I mean?" she said.

The power did go out a short time later, while Bobby and I were washing the dishes. We had to finish by lamplight. Jeff and Grandpa made the fire, and we settled down next to the crackling flames as the thunder rumbled and the rain beat down on the roof.

"So what ghost story would you like to hear?" Grandpa asked us. As if he didn't know.

"Tell us about Blackbeard," Jeff said immediately.

"Tell us about Blackbeard's ghost," I corrected him.

"I want to know about Teach's light," said Bobby.

"Well now, I think I can cover all that," Grandpa said with a smile. He passed us the bowl of popcorn and began his story.

"Edward Teach was once an ordinary English privateer, who had served in the Navy during Queen Anne's War with Spain. But when peace came in 1713, Teach became a pirate."

"Blackbeard," Bobby said happily.

"Yes indeed," Grandpa said. "Edward Teach was a tall man, and he had a very long black beard that covered most of his face and extended down to his waist. He'd tie his beard up in pigtails adorned with black ribbons. He wore a bandolier over his shoulders with three braces of pistols, and sometimes he would hang two slow-burning cannon fuses from his fur cap to wreath his head in black smoke. Occasionally, he'd even set fire to his rum using gunpowder, and he would drink it, flames and all.

"For more than two years, Blackbeard terrorized the sailors of the Atlantic and the Caribbean, ambushing ships and stealing their cargo, killing those who opposed him, often attacking in the dim light of dawn or dusk when his pirate ship was most difficult to see. He would sail under the flag of a country friendly to the nationality of the ship he was attacking, and then hoist his pirate flag at the last moment. When prisoners surrendered willingly, he spared them. When they did not, his magnanimity failed. One man refused to give up a diamond ring he was wearing, and the pirate cut the ring off, finger and all."

I gave a gasp of fright. For a moment, I could almost see the prisoner's finger flying through the air, the blood spurting from his hand. Grandpa glanced quickly at me and changed the tone of his story a little.

"Blackbeard had a way with the ladies. They seemed to find him attractive in spite of—or maybe because of—his marauding ways. Over the years, Blackbeard married thirteen different women. No sooner had he left one wife behind to go pirating than he became enamored of another. The only woman who scorned him was the daughter of Governor Eden. Eden was governor of North Carolina in those days, and he got a share of Blackbeard's plunder in exchange for ignoring the pirate's illegal activities. But Eden's daughter did not care for Blackbeard. She was engaged to another man, and spurned Blackbeard's suit. So Blackbeard hunted down her fiancé, cut off his hand, and threw him into the sea to drown. He then sent a jewel casket to Miss Eden. When she opened it, she found the severed hand of her dead lover."

Bobby's eyes grew round as he envisioned Miss Eden opening the jeweled box containing the severed hand.

"What happened to her?" Bobby asked.

"She grew ill and died," Grandpa said gravely.

"Once, Blackbeard blockaded Charleston, South Carolina, with his ships, taking many wealthy citizens hostage until the townspeople met his ransom. Another time, Blackbeard ran aground one of his own ships, the Queen Anne's Revenge. Some say he did it on purpose because he wanted to break up the pirate fleet and steal the booty for himself.

"Then in November of 1718, Blackbeard retreated to his favorite hideaway off Ocracoke Island, where he hosted a wild pirate party with drinking, dancing, and large bonfires. The party lasted for days, and several North Carolina citizens, tired of the way Governor Eden ignored the pirate, sent word to Governor Alexander Spotswood of Virginia. Governor Spotswood immediately ordered two sloops, commanded by Lieutenant Robert Maynard of the Royal Navy, to go to Ocracoke and capture the pirate.

"On November 21, 1718, Maynard engaged Blackbeard in a terrible battle. One of Maynard's ships was between Blackbeard and freedom. Blackbeard sailed his ship, the Adventure, in toward shore. It looked like the pirate was going to crash his ship, but at the last second it eased through a narrow channel.

"One of the Navy ships went aground on a sandbar when it tried to pursue the Adventure. Blackbeard fired his cannon at the remaining ship, and many of Maynard's men were killed. The rest Maynard ordered below the deck under cover of the gun smoke, to fool the pirates into thinking they had won. When the pirates boarded the ship, Maynard and his men attacked. Although outnumbered, the pirates put up a bloody fight. Blackbeard and Maynard came face to face. They both shot at each other. Blackbeard's shot missed Maynard, but Maynard's bullet hit the pirate. Blackbeard swung his cutlass and managed to snap off Maynard's sword blade near the hilt. As Blackbeard prepared to deliver the deathblow, one of Maynard's men cut Blackbeard's throat from behind. Blackbeard's blow missed its mark, barely skinning Maynard's knuckles. Infuriated, Blackbeard fought on as the blood spouted from his neck. Maynard and his men rushed the pirate. It took a total of five gunshots and about twenty cuts before Blackbeard fell down dead."

"Wow," Jeff breathed.

"Edward Teach was quite a fierce man," said Grandpa. "Maynard seemed to think that the only way to ensure that Blackbeard was dead was to remove his head. They hung the head from the bowsprit and threw the pirate's body overboard. As the body hit the water, the head hanging from the bowsprit shouted, 'Come on Edward!' and the headless body swam three times around the ship before sinking to the bottom.

"From that day to this, the headless ghost of Blackbeard has haunted Teach's Hole. Whenever the wind blows inland, you can still hear Blackbeard's ghost tramping up and down. It carries a lantern through the moonless night, roaring, 'Where's my head?!' Whenever folks see a strange light coming from the shore on the Pamlico Sound side of Ocracoke Island, they call it Teach's light." Grandpa smiled at Bobby.

"And sometimes," he continued, looking at me, "you can see Blackbeard's headless ghost floating on the surface of the water, or swimming around and around and around Teach's Hole, glowing just underneath the water, searching for his head. For Blackbeard is as proud in death as he was in life, and he doesn't want to meet the Devil or his crewmates in hell without a head on his shoulders."

Bobby, Jeff, and I all shivered as Grandpa finished his story. The thunder had died away, and the rain beat steadily on the roof.

"Time for bed," Grandma said, breaking the spell. We all groaned, but got up.

"Tomorrow night, if it's clear, I will take you to Teach's Hole," Grandpa promised as we trooped upstairs to prepare for bed.

The rain had ceased by the time I closed the bedroom door for the night. I went to the window and looked out toward the sea. In my mind, I could picture Blackbeard fighting Maynard on the deck of the ship, his blood spurting out as he fought to his death. Then I thought I saw a light. I opened my window and leaned out, getting my nightgown wet. I strained my ears.

Was it him? Was it Teach? The wind rustled the leaves on the trees, and the night was dark again. I sighed, closed the window, and went to bed.

14

The Log Cabin

MONTGOMERY COUNTY, ARKANSAS

Now I've heard tell of an old, weather-beaten log cabin way back in the woods of Arkansas that is supposed to be as haunted as a place can be. Folks from miles around claim that ghosts, a lot of ghosts, make that old log cabin home. There's not a preacher in this whole world who can make them ghosts leave. There's not a barn raising or Ladies Aid meeting or after-church gathering where folks don't discuss the haunts in the old log cabin. Everyone has heard of someone who's had a ghostly encounter there.

Even hunters who find themselves in that area after dark don't try to spend the night in that old log cabin, even if it means they have to walk several more miles until they find another place to roost for the night. Course, there are always daredevils who try to spend the night in the cabin. And it's always the same old story. Round about midnight, they hear a moaning and a rumbling and a shrieking such as would scare the living daylights out of anyone, and they start a-running for their lives.

Now one of these men, who went by the name of Fred, was telling his story round a campfire one night. He summed up his

THE LOG CABIN

tale by saying that there wasn't a man alive who could stay in that there haunted cabin from dusk until dawn.

"Yes there is too," a man called Uncle Sam spoke up promptly. "You just give me fifty dollars, a frying pan, a hunk of meat, and a loaf of bread, and I'll stay there from dark till noon."

The friends all laughed, but Uncle Sam was serious. So they gave Uncle Sam his fifty dollars, his frying pan, his meat, his loaf of bread, and they escorted him to the edge of the clearing where the old log cabin stood. Then they went back to their campfire as Uncle Sam marched up to the door and went into the small cabin.

There was only one room with a rough fireplace and a few rickety chairs. Uncle Sam made a fire and settled himself in a chair to enjoy his pipe. When it grew near midnight, Uncle Sam decided it was time to fry up his pork. He put the frying pan on the fire, set the pork in to sizzle, and then settled back into his chair for another smoke. The small cabin filled with the delicious smell of frying pork, and Uncle Sam crossed his legs and settled deeper into his seat with a happy sigh. He patted the pocket where he had put the money and reckoned that it was the easiest fifty dollars he had ever made.

Something stirred in the shadows. Uncle Sam, still lost in a pleasant dream of spending all the money on women and whiskey, didn't notice the movement. He started in surprise when he saw a wrinkled black creature about the size of a hare scurry out onto the hearth. It had small black wings on its back, an evil-looking face, and glowing red eyes. The tiny imp spat right across the frying pan into the back of the fire. Uncle Sam frowned. Now that ain't nice at all, he mused, messing with a man's meal.

The imp looked up at Uncle Sam with its glowing red eyes.

"There's nobody here but you and me tonight," the imp said conversationally.

Uncle Sam's whole attention was centered on the meat sizzling in the frying pan. He was trying to figure out if that imp had spat into the fire or into the meat. Uncle Sam didn't take no notice of the imp's words. Leaning forward, he stirred the meat in the frying pan. It looked all right, and it still smelled delicious.

The imp was not pleased. It spat into the fire again, right next to the frying pan. Uncle Sam sat up with a jerk. He was furious. He had been looking forward to his meal all evening, and now this pesky imp had almost ruined it. Uncle Sam swatted at the imp, shouting, "Don't you spit in my meat!"

Quick as lightning, the imp kicked out at the frying pan, spilling the meat into the fire. Then it lunged up at Uncle Sam, clawing him between the eyes. Uncle Sam reeled back in his chair in pain as the imp returned to its place on the hearth. There was a moment of heavy silence. Uncle Sam clutched his bleeding forehead and looked numbly at the imp. Then the creature turned its red eyes on Uncle Sam again and said, "There's nobody here but you and me tonight."

Uncle Sam stared, mesmerized, into the imp's eyes. He felt as if he were falling into the pit of hell. Flames flickered at the edge of his vision. Around him, he could hear the unearthly moans and the terrible shrieks of the damned, rising louder and louder. His forehead began to throb. The imp's words echoed repeatedly through his head until he thought he would lose his mind: "There's nobody here but you and me. There's nobody here but you and me."

Still clutching his bleeding forehead, Uncle Sam shot up out of his rickety chair.

"I-I-I'll not be here long," he stammered, and rushed for the door. As the door slammed behind him, Uncle Sam heard the imp give an unearthly screech. Through the clear night, he could hear the sound of claws scraping at the wood of the door. Uncle Sam ran for his life.

Uncle Sam would have kept running right past the campsite if his friends hadn't stopped him.

"What happened?" demanded Fred as the group surrounded the terrified man.

Speechless, Uncle Sam thrust the fifty dollars into Fred's hand, elbowed his way out of the group, and ran the rest of the way home. Uncle Sam rarely spoke to anyone about what he saw that night. And he never went near the old log cabin again.

15

The Woman in Black

I was just a young lad in those days, living with my family in Savannah. My brother and me, we liked to walk over and see my mother's sister who lived in the next town. The shortest way to my aunt's house was past the cemetery. My older brother Teddy didn't mind walking next to all them dead folks, but it made me nervous. I always made excuses to go home early 'cause I didn't want to pass that cemetery at night. My brother, he just laughed at me and told me there was nothing to be scared of.

Well, one night we stayed and stayed at my aunt's house until it was well past dark. I was plumb scared to walk home past that cemetery, but my brother just laughed and waved the cane he used when his rheumatism started acting up.

"I'll protect you from the ghosts, Collier," he said. "I'll hit 'em with my stick."

"Very funny," I replied. I said goodbye to my aunt and followed Teddy out the door. It was one of those nights that's real dark 'cause the moon had already set. There were hardly any lights coming from the houses, and even the lightning bugs weren't out. I didn't like it one bit, having to walk home in the dark, but Teddy was already hobbling ahead of me, leaning on

THE WOMAN IN BLACK

his stick 'cause his leg was bothering him something fierce. So I followed along. The only thing worse than walking home in the dark is walking home in the dark alone.

"Wait for me!" I called to Teddy. I caught up with him right quick and we started walking along the fence. We'd only gone about a hundred yards when we caught sight of a lady coming toward us in the light from one dim street lamp. She was a real pretty lady. She was wearing a fancy black silk dress that rustled as she walked, and she had a long black veil over her face. Teddy and I were real surprised to see her 'cause we both thought the street was empty. It seemed like she appeared from nowhere. Gave me goose bumps, but Teddy weren't spooked a bit. He gave the woman a fancy bow like he always did when he saw a pretty face.

The woman came right up to us and asked, "Are you going around the fence?"

Something about her voice made me feel chilled to the bone. I stared hard at her, but she seemed as real as Ted and me. I decided I was just thinking crazy 'cause we were near that cemetery.

"We are indeed, madam," Teddy said grandly, tapping his stick for emphasis. He was talking in that learned manner he used with the gals. I rolled my eyes.

"You are not afraid?" asked the woman.

"No, madam," Teddy said. "Collier is, but he is just a little fellow."

I resented his words.

"I am not afraid," I said stoutly, ignoring my shaking knees and the goose bumps on my arms. There was something spooky about that woman's voice. It had an odd echo as if she were speaking in a cave. But she was mighty pretty, her face all misty behind the black veil.

"Perhaps you would let me walk with you," said the woman, "since you are not afraid."

"It would be our pleasure," Teddy said, swelling with pride. "You don't need to be afraid with us, madam."

"Indeed," said the woman, turning to walk along the fence next to Teddy. I lagged behind. I couldn't shake the feeling that something was wrong. Teddy was still talking grandly to the woman, trying to impress her with his wit, when I saw something over the cemetery fence. A small, white shape was rising out of the ground. It looked like mist at first, but it gradually became solid. Teddy must have seen it too, 'cause he suddenly stopped talking and stood still. I nearly bumped into him since I was looking at that misty thing and not where I was walking. The woman in black stopped with us, and we all watched as the misty shape solidified into what looked like a huge white rat.

Then the rat sprang forward and ran straight toward us. Teddy and I jumped back in terror, but the woman in black didn't move. For several terrible seconds we watched that white rat coming closer, closer. Then the woman picked up her black silk skirts and ran to meet it. The white rat sprang up into her arms and then sank right through her chest. I caught a glimpse of her face through the veil. It was all sunken in like the face of a corpse. She laughed, a horrible high-pitched sound. Then the earth seemed to open below her feet and she sank down and down.

Teddy let out a shriek that was almost as terrible as the ghoul-woman's cry. He dropped his stick and started running as if he'd never suffered from rheumatism a day in his life. I was right on his heels. We never stopped running till we got home.

After that, we always took the long way to my aunt's house and made sure we left before dark.

16

The Handshake

Polly was the sweetest, prettiest girl in Goldsboro, yes sir. All the local boys were chasing her, and quite a number of the fellows from the surrounding countryside were too. All the girls were jealous of Polly 'cause they didn't have no sweethearts to take them to the local dances, but even they couldn't help liking her. Polly would give someone the shirt off her back if they needed it. That's just the way she was. Of course, the girls all wanted Polly to choose her man so things could go back to normal. But Polly was picky. None of the local boys suited her, and neither did the fellows from the backcountry.

Then one day, George Dean came home from university, and Polly was smitten. He was handsome, tall, and mysterious. He didn't chase her like the other fellows. He seemed to favor the other girls. For weeks Polly fumed as George played beau to first one pretty girl then another. Didn't he see her at all? She was in a real tizzy by the time handsome George Dean wandered up to her front porch one evening and asked if she'd care to take a stroll down the lane. Polly sniffed and acted haughty at first, but finally she allowed that a stroll might not come amiss.

THE HANDSHAKE

From that moment on, Polly and George were inseparable. You couldn't turn around without bumping into them at one social event or another. Polly completely dropped all her other beaus, much to the relief of the local girls, and soon the town was filled with the laughter of many courting couples. The Saturday night dances were particularly popular, and it was at one of those that George proposed and Polly accepted. There was great rejoicing—particularly among the eligible young females, who'd been afeared of what might happen if Polly broke it off with George.

A day was set, and Polly started making preparations for the wedding and shopping for items to fill her new home. George wasn't too interested in all the fripperies and wedding details. He left the womenfolk to get on with it and started spending time down at the pool hall with some of his buddies. And that's where he met Helene, the owner's saucy daughter. She had bold black eyes and ruby-red lips, and a bad-girl air that fascinated George. He spent more and more time at the pool hall, and less and less time with Polly, who finally noticed in spite of all the hustle and bustle.

She made a few inquiries, and Cindy—a girl who'd lost her favorite beau to Polly a few years back—told her all about Helene. In detail.

Of course, Polly was furious. She immediately confronted George with the story, and he couldn't deny it. Suddenly, George had to toe the mark. His pool-hall visits were over, and he spent every free hour he wasn't at work by her side. That didn't sit well with George, but his family backed Polly up, so he went along with it.

The day of the wedding dawned clear and bright. Polly and her bridesmaids went to the church to get dressed in their finery, whispering excitedly together. The guests filled the sanctuary, and the pastor and the best man waited patiently in the antechamber for the groom's arrival. They waited. And waited. And waited some more. But George didn't come.

The best man hurried into the sanctuary to talk to the groom's father, who hustled back to the house right quick to check on his son. Still no George. Had he been in an accident? Was he hurt? No one knew the answer.

George's brothers went searching for him, calling in at the police, at the hospital. His youngest brother even went to the pool hall. And that's when he found out that Helene was missing too. Helene's youngest sister told George's youngest brother that she'd seen them leave the pool hall together about an hour before the wedding. So that was that.

With dread, Polly's mother went to tell her daughter what had happened. Polly, all bright and shining and lovely in her long white dress and soft wedding veil, turned pale when her mother broke the news.

"It couldn't be. George would never do that!" she exclaimed. She stared blankly at her mother, swayed a bit, and then stiffened, grabbing her left arm as a sudden pain ripped through it. She was dead from a massive heart attack before she hit the floor.

And so Polly's wedding became—in essence—Polly's wake. Her family was furious. George's family was furious and embarrassed. And the guests were furious too. George's unthinking actions had killed the sweetest, prettiest girl in Goldsboro. If he was going to jilt her, the gossips all agreed, he should have done it privately. He shouldn't have left her at the altar.

A few days later Polly was buried in the churchyard, still wearing her white wedding dress and veil. The whole town came to the funeral and wept at the passing of such a beautiful young girl. George and Helene, who had spent the week happily honeymooning in the Outer Banks, arrived home at the very moment that the black-clad crowd exited the churchyard. Their arrival caused a commotion. The minister had to pull Polly's father off George before he killed him. And George's family disowned him right there in the street in front of everyone. Even the attorneys at the law office where George worked turned him away, knowing that no one in town would do business with them as long as George remained on their staff.

Helene's family was equally embarrassed. No one was visiting the pool hall anymore, and it looked like they would have to move away from town. They refused to open their door to their daughter and her new husband. Only Helene's youngest sister relented enough to open the upper window of the pool hall and speak to her sister. She dropped a bundle of clothes down to Helene and then slammed the window shut immediately afterward to make her position clear. So George and Helene left town in disgrace to make a new life for themselves elsewhere.

Life moved on. The scandal grew cold, and new ones took its place as new interests arose among the young people and the gossips. Polly and George and Helene were forgotten. Then, a year after Polly's death, George's father passed and was buried in the local churchyard just a few plots away from the girl who had almost become his daughter-in-law. This event triggered gossip about the fatal wedding day. For a few days the story of Polly and George was revived and much discussed.

Everyone in town turned out for the funeral of the elder Mr. Dean. Everyone was waiting to see if George would show his face. But George was too clever for them. He waited at an inn outside of town until it was dark, and then he went to the churchyard to pay his last respects to his father.

George Junior stood by the freshly dug grave and told his father that things weren't going so well. His old law firm had refused to give him a reference, and word of Polly's death had reached those at his former university who might have once helped him. So he was working as a farmhand, barely able to feed and clothe himself and his wife, who flagrantly chased after other men.

As he unburdened himself at his father's graveside, George heard a sweet female voice calling his name. "George. Sweetheart." George looked up in sudden hope. Was that his mother, come to forgive him? But no, the voice was pitched too high to be his mother, who sang contralto in the church choir.

"George," the voice called again. Puzzled, George turned toward the sound. And then he saw, rising up from a grassy mound under a spreading oak tree, a figure in a long white gown and a soft veil. Her eyes and her lips were yellow flames beneath the veil, and the rotted wedding dress glowed with a white-yellow light. It was Polly.

George's body stiffened, shudders of fear coursing up and down his arms and legs. Every hair on his neck prickled, and bile rose up into his throat until he retched and threw up on his father's grave. He put a shaking hand to his mouth and staggered backward, the other hand outstretched to ward off the specter floating toward him.

The spectral bride cackled with angry laughter and swooped forward until her hand closed over George's outstretched one in a terrible parody of a handshake. The grip of the spectral bride was so cold that it burned the skin, and so hard that the bones crunched as she squeezed. "Come along into the church, George," the glowing bride whispered. Through the veil, George could see maggots crawling in and out of Polly's flaming eye sockets.

"Nooo! Polly, no!" George screamed in terror, but he could not wrench his hand free. The ghost dragged him step by halting step toward the front door of the church. His hand was a red-hot agony of pain, though the rest of his body was shaking with cold. The agony was spreading now, up his arm to his shoulder.

"No!" George gave a final cry of despair and wrenched again at his hand. And suddenly, he was free. The spectral bride gave a roar of rage as George ran pell-mell down the church lane and out into the street.

"You're mine, George Dean! If not in this world, then in the next," the spectral bride howled after him. Her glowing form swelled upward until it was taller than the treetops. George looked back once and fell headlong when he saw the massive form with its flaming yellow eyes and lips and the moldering rags of its white wedding dress. He picked himself up, terror lending him speed. Clutching his aching hand, he ran all the way back to the inn.

By the time George reached his room, the fiery pain in his hand and arm was seeping through his entire body. He rang desperately for the housemaid and begged her to send for a doctor. Then he fell into bed and stared at his hand, which was black and withered, as if it had been scorched long ago by a fire. Black and red streaks were climbing up his arm so fast that he could almost see them move.

George was unconscious when the doctor arrived, and the swelling was already extending into his chest and neck. There was nothing the physician could do. The injury was too severe and had spread too far. Within two days George was dead. Polly had gotten her man at last.

17

I Know Moonrise

Mama told me I should never walk along the marsh shortcut that led from our plantation to the town of Brunswick. She said it was dangerous and I'd get myself killed if I didn't listen to her. At first this restriction didn't bother me none. I had plenty of work to do in the forge helping Pa, who was the local blacksmith. My tasks kept me near home most of the time. But when I grew older, the fellers started laughing at me, saying I was a baby because my folks wouldn't let me take the marsh shortcut. I got so mad I told Mama to her face that I wasn't listening to her no more. She gave me a terrible scold and sent me to bed without supper. I was so mad over the whole thing I could have spit nails! She treated me like a baby and I was thirteen years old!

It was Pa, still smelling of charcoal and smoke from the forge, who came and told me why Mama was so scared of the marsh path. "We thought it best to wait until you had grown some afore telling you the story of the marsh path," Pa said. "Yer mama's little sister disappeared in the marsh a long time ago. She was taking the shortcut to the old pond to gather some

I KNOW MOONRISE

firewood, and she never came back. They found her straw hat floating in the stagnant water, but they never found her body."

"I ain't gonna fall into the water like Mama's sister what passed," I protested. "I'm thirteen. Big enough to walk alone in the marsh."

"That ain't it, son," Pa said. "I know you're big enough to walk the marsh path without falling in. It's . . . " He rubbed his face with a sweaty palm, eyes troubled. Chills ran up my arms. I'd never seen Pa at a loss for words before. "It's the spirit of yer little aunt," Pa said finally. "She comes to the marsh path some evenings and she . . . she sings."

Color drained from my face and my arms grew goosefleshed. "She's a ghost?" I gasped, clutching the blanket with tense fingers.

"Not just a ghost, son," Pa said. "You heard about the Jack Ma Lantern?"

"'Course, Pa," I said. "It's an evil spirit that tries to drown you in the marsh. You can see his lantern flashing sometimes at night. That's why all the fellers wear their jackets inside out when they walk through the marsh."

"That's right," said Pa. "Yer little aunt, she's kind of like the Jack Ma Lantern. After she drowned, her ghost started floating over the marsh at night, singing softly of death and the grave. She's lonesome and wants her family to join her, so she lures them into the water with her song." Pa swallowed hard and continued: "It's safe fer your buddies to walk that path 'cause they ain't family. But if you go there, the ghost will come fer you."

I pulled the covers up around my eyes, and my whole body turned to shivers as Pa described the little girl in the swamp.

Pa continued, "The ghost almost got yer mama, back in our courtin' days. If I hadn't been with her, yer mama would have drowned. She was waist deep in the water, following that singing voice afore I realized she'd left my side. I hauled her out of the mud and threw her over my shoulder, dripping gunk and weed all over my new shirt. Yer mama kicked and hollered something terrible, trying to get away from me so she could follow her little sister's ghost. The spirit floated beside me as I jogged down that trail with yer mama over my shoulder, singing 'I Know Moonrise' in a sweet voice that made my body shake all over. Yer mama screamed at me, wanting to go to her little sister, but I held on tight. As soon as I stepped off the marsh path, the ghost vanished and yer mama went limp. Fer a moment I thought she was dead, but she'd just fainted when the ghost disappeared. That was the last time anyone in yer family ever walked the marsh path."

I blinked. He was right. I couldn't remember seeing anyone in my family on the marsh path. Grandpa, Grandma, my aunts and uncles and grown-up cousins, they all used the road. Pa saw realization dawn on my face and rubbed the top of my head.

"You stay away from the marsh, son," he said.

I should have listened to Pa. But it was easy to forget the ghost in the long days of summer as the fellers and I rambled around the countryside after the day's work was done. I sure wasn't thinking about it the day Jimmy and I were caught in Brunswick after sunset. "My pa's going to be sore at me if I miss dinner," Jimmy said. "We better hurry." We raced down the road toward the plantation. Suddenly Jimmy swerved toward the marsh, and I realized he meant to take the shortcut.

I stared after my buddy, torn between speed and safety. I should take the road. But Jimmy was there, so chances were good that the ghost wouldn't come 'cause he weren't family. Besides, I reasoned, the little aunt never met me, so why would she want me to join her on the other side? Jimmy's head appeared around a tussocky bend in the path. "Come on," he called impatiently. I whipped off my jacket and turned it inside out to keep Jack Ma Lantern (and my aunt) away. Then I raced down the marsh path after Jimmy.

It was getting real dark, and phantom lights were popping up in the distance while the sky was still turning from gray to black. The wind swished through the marsh grasses, all whisper-whisper-whisper. Jimmy hugged his arms around his body. He didn't like the sound of that wind.

We were walking single file along the path with Jimmy in the lead when a bullfrog bellowed beside us. We shouted in fear, nearly toppling into the water beside the path. Then we laughed nervously, clutching at each other to steady ourselves.

"I thought that frog was the Jack Ma Lantern!" Jimmy exclaimed. With a grin he shook me off and headed down the path. I paused for a moment to admire the moon, which was rising over the treetops, making a glittering path across the still water.

As I turned to follow Jimmy, the air around me grew cold till my whole body shook with chills. Out of the silvery moon-sparkle there came a childlike figure that danced and floated above the dark water like a will-o'-the-wisp. I gasped, my throat tight with fear. I called to Jimmy, just a yard in front of me, but he didn't hear me, and I knew he couldn't see the spirit floating toward us across the marsh. My legs shook so bad that I couldn't walk. The silvery will-o'-the-wisp shimmered and grew until I saw a shining little girl in a straw hat. My mouth opened and shut like a dying fish. Puffs of freezing air formed in front of my nostrils as the little girl drew closer to the marsh path. Then she started to sing.

I know moonrise, I know star-rise; Lay dis body down.
I walk in de moonlight, I walk in de starlight,
To lay dis body down.
I'll walk in de graveyard, I'll walk through de graveyard,
To lay dis body down.
I'll lie in de grave and stretch out my arms;
Lay dis body down.
I go to de judgment in de evenin' of de day,
When I lay dis body down.
And my soul and your soul will meet in de day,
When I lay dis body down.

Suddenly I relaxed, lovely pictures floating through my head. I saw myself winning awards at school and studying hard so that I won a scholarship to university. Then I saw myself as an important lawyer, earning enough money to buy a mansion with a big fancy garden in back.

I was so excited by this vision that I ran to the cabin where I lived with Mama and Pa to tell them the great news about my future. Mama stood at the far side of the room and I called out to her, but she didn't hear me. She held a hand to her ear and beckoned me closer. I hurried toward her, splashing through water that came to my knees, my waist, my chest. There was only one thought in my head. I must reach Mama and tell her I was going to university to be a scholar. I shouted the words as loud as I could, but my mouth filled with water and I choked. "Mama!" I called, stretching strangely heavy arms toward her. She reached toward me, and I was overwhelmed by the stink of stagnant marsh water. My heart froze in fear, for Mama's eyes were glowing silver. The world went dark.

I woke gasping as someone pounded me on the chest. I choked and threw up all over the person who was thumping my ribs. The muddy water coming from my mouth tasted as foul as it smelled. I vomited again, this time vomiting my lunch along with the marsh water. I could hear Jimmy blubbering in the background but felt too ill to open my eyes. Then I heard Pa's voice: "Son? You all right? Son!"

I opened my eyes and saw my pa's face above me in the shimmering moonlight. I was soaked to the skin, and my whole body trembled with cold and shock. "I saw her, Pa," I gasped. "She sang to me. She sang. . . . "

I lost consciousness again. When I woke I was in my bed and Mama was holding my hand and weeping. I stared up at her, vowing then and there that I would never again do anything to make my mama cry. I squeezed her hand and she looked up, startled, when she realized I was awake. She hugged me so tight I could barely breathe and scolded me something fierce for disobeying her. I promised her that I would never walk the marsh path again, and I kept that promise.

But after that night I had to leave the rice fields whenever the workers sang "I Know Moonrise." Hearing the tune made my whole body shake and my mouth taste of rotting marsh water.

18

Fiddler's Dram

DUKEDOM, TENNESSEE

I reckon that no one who attended the jailhouse concert and fiddle contest ever forgot it. I know I never did.

I was just a young chap back in those days, but I was already county clerk, and I had ambitions to become a judge. I was at the county court the day the wall of the jailhouse fell out. This was a real tragedy, though I suppose the criminals in Dukedom didn't mind, because the county court didn't have enough money to fix the jail. All the prominent citizens gathered round the scene of the disaster, wondering what to do. Finally, I suggested we get up a fiddling contest. Folks around Dukedom would come from miles around to hear a good fiddler play, and we could raise the money in no time flat.

"Great idea, Fred," Coot Kersey said heartily. He was the best fiddle player in Dukedom.

Everyone nodded enthusiastically, and the doctor said, "We'll have to notify Ples Haslock."

This brought cheers from everyone but Coot. In those days, we had fiddlers who could bring tears to the eyes of the most hardened criminal. They could make their fiddles sing, screech,

FIDDLER'S DRAM

cry, and play the sweetest music this side of the heavenly realms. And the best of the best was Ples Haslock.

Ples Haslock drew a crowd every time he picked up his fiddle. He fiddled for all the local parties and dances, sometimes going fifty miles or more because the folks in these parts figured a party wasn't a party without Ples and his fiddle. I can still see him in my mind, calling out the figures for the local square dances, his long face solemn except for a sparkle in his light blue eyes. He always looked into the distance as he fiddled, as if he could see wondrous things just out of sight.

Ples was young and handsome and the girls vied for his attention, much to the chagrin of the rest of us young bloods. But I think Ples was married to his fiddle, because he didn't pay the girls any attention. I once heard him say that as long as he had his fiddle and a place to tap his toe, he didn't need anything else in all creation. Maybe that was true.

Ples had taught himself to play the fiddle when he was quite young. His daddy had traded an old horse for a bunch of junk being peddled by an Irish Gypsy, and Ples found a fiddle box among the crates. Ples made some strings for the old fiddle box, and soon he was playing better than all the other fiddlers in the area.

When Ples's daddy died, Ples inherited the old family house. But he wasn't home much. Ples liked to travel around, gossiping and visiting with folks. He was welcomed with open arms, not just for his fiddling, but also for his stories, which could keep a family spellbound into the wee hours of the night, and for the news he brought of the latest happenings.

Ples stayed with my folks a few times, and I remember the way he used his fiddle to help him tell stories. Ples could make his fiddle sound like the buzz of a mosquito, the grumbling voice of an old woman, a peeping chicken, or a mockingbird in a tree. By the time Ples was done with one of his tales, we were either breathless with excitement or lying on the floor laughing. Then he would play us a tune that would bring tears to our eyes. We were devastated when he left, but Ples never stayed anywhere for long.

Just hearing that Ples was going to play drew large crowds to the local fiddling contests, but it got so that it was hard to get any other fiddlers to sign up for a contest. Once they knew Ples was going to fiddle, they knew there was no contest. Ples always walked off with the Fiddler's Dram—a gallon of fine drinking whiskey—at every fiddling contest in the district. Folks started offering a jug to the second place winner so other fiddlers would sign up for the contests. The fiddlers all vied with one another over that second jug; they never bothered about the first one. No one ever beat Ples, and well they knew it.

"I hear that Ples is down with heart dropsy," Coot Kersey said to the folks gathered around the collapsed jailhouse wall. "Maybe he can't come this time."

"Or so you hope, eh Coot?" Everyone laughed, even Coot.

"I'm heading over that way on business tomorrow," I said. "I'll stop by and notify Ples of the contest."

"You're a good man, Fred," ol' Doc Smith said.

Everyone decided that the jailhouse benefit fiddling contest would take place two weeks from that Monday, and the crowd dispersed. In the morning I drove over to Ples Haslock's place and stopped my wagon in front of the house. The house—a one-room shack, really—was looking pretty dilapidated. The shingles were beginning to curl up on the roof, and some of the clapboards had dropped right off.

"Ples Haslock," I called out. "You home, Ples?"

No one answered from the house. I climbed the shaky steps to the porch.

"Who's there?" Ples called from inside.

"It's Fred Bennett from Dukedom."

"Come on in," Ples called at once. "I haven't seen you in a coon's age. How's your folks?"

I went into the one-room house, which was filled with clutter—old clothes, pots, pans, and junk of all sorts. Ples was lying in bed at the far end of the room, under a heap of old quilts, his fiddle beside him. I was shocked at how pale and ill Ples looked. His face had shrunken and was tinged with green, and there were big liver splotches on his face and hands.

"My folks are doing well," I said. "How are you feeling, Ples?"

"Feelin' a might poorly," Ples said, his long fingers plucking gently at the strings of his fiddle. "I don't reckon I know what I'd do if it weren't for my kind neighbors. The women bring me things to eat three times a day and sit talking with me. The menfolk check up on me at night to make sure I ain't fell out of bed or be ailin' and need help. Between visits, I just lay here and play my fiddle."

"I heard you were ailing," I said, dropping into a chair beside him.

"That's a fact," said Ples. "The heart dropsy runs in the Haslock family. I've been having a bit of a rough time, but I aim to be up and about soon."

"That's good news, Ples," I said, wondering if I should tell him about the fiddle contest. I decided it couldn't hurt anything, so I told him all about the jail wall falling in, making a story of it like he used to tell me stories when I was small. When I got to the part about the fiddle contest, Ples perked up.

"I'll be there for sure!" Ples was pleased as punch. "When that roll is called up yonder in Dukedom, I'll be there for certain!"

I visited with Ples for quite a while, and reluctantly took leave of him. He looked so ill that I wasn't sure if I would ever see him again. But I said lightly, "We'll be looking for you at the benefit, Ples."

"Get that Fiddler's Dram ready," said Ples with a tired grin. "I'm aiming to win it!"

The night of the benefit, nearly everyone in Dukedom turned out in their Sunday best. The contest was being held at the schoolhouse and everyone hurried in to get a good seat. I sat with my girl near the front, since I was one of the sponsors. The room was filled with the typical sort of frolicking that goes with such a big event: old folks gossiping, boys and girls running about, young men talking loudly and showing off for the girls, who sneaked glances at them and giggled. I sat next to my girl and tried to look nonchalant, even though my little sister kept turning around to stick her tongue out at us.

When folks started getting restless, Judge Huley Dunlap hurried out on the stage and announced that the contest was about to start. Everyone settled down. Into the relative silence, the judge read the names of the seven fiddlers who would compete. Ples Haslock's name was not among them.

Everyone started yelling: "What about Ples? Where's Ples?"

"Well," Judge Dunlap said. "We've been hoping he'd make it here tonight, but he's been feeling poorly and it's a long way. I reckon he couldn't stand up to the trip. If anybody wants their admission fee back, they can get it at the door."

There was quite a bit of grumbling, but everyone stayed in their seats. The seven fiddlers came out on the stage and took their seats. Everyone in the crowd knew that the first five fiddlers didn't stand a chance. They were just run-of-the-mill types who sat around and sawed at the strings. No, with Ples Haslock out of the running, the contest was between Coot Kersey and Old Rob Reddin.

Well, the first five fiddlers played and no one paid them any special attention. They were as average as could be. Then came Coot's turn. Now Coot looked more like an old turkey than anything else. His head bobbed when he walked, his nose was hooked like a beak, and his hair flopped about. He was greeted with shouts and laughter as he stood up and took a bow.

But Coot was a serious fiddler. He got his fiddle set just right before he started playing a rousing rendition of "Leather Britches." He sawed and fiddled and played stunts on the strings until sweat poured off of him. When he finished, the crowd gave him a rousing hand-clap.

Then Old Rob Reddin waddled forward. If Coot resembled a turkey, Old Rob looked like a round red ball with a small bobble of a head on top. Old Rob was the funniest man in town. Not a word could he say without making someone laugh. The crowd grinned just to see him, and my girl muffled giggles in her hands. When Old Rob played the fiddle, it was as much acting as playing. He winked at his wife, who was sitting near the front and said, "Hold on to your hats, folks! I aim to drive wild!"

The crowd cheered. Then Old Rob started fiddling "Hell Turned Loose in Georgia." It was quite a performance. Old Rob bent low with the low notes, lifted his eyebrows to the ceiling when the fiddle played high, and every once in a while he'd throw his bow right up into the air and catch it again. As he caught his bow, he'd shout out phrases like, "Ladies, where was your husband Saturday night?"

The crowd was shouting and stomping and whistling when Old Rob finished. Old Rob had won hands down.

The entire audience was watching Old Rob caper about, which was why no one saw Ples Haslock until he had already played a few lines of "Poor Wayfaring Stranger." All heads turned to look at the stage as the sweet sounds filled the hall. We were astonished to see Ples, sitting in the fiddler's chair, tapping his foot softly, his head nodding in time to the tune. Ples looked all pale and sickly, but he had made it just in time to play in the contest. The room rustled as everyone settled quietly into their seats. No one wanted to miss a note of the haunting song.

It was nine o'clock when Ples started playing. He played for over an hour, straight fiddle playing from the heart, with none of the stunts and shouts of Coot and Old Rob. Ples Haslock could make people laugh and weep when he played, but for those of us who heard him play that night, it was more like entering into a dream. Ples's music made me feel like there was something beautiful just beyond my grasp. My girl, seated beside me, told me later that she felt like she heard the voice of her dead mother telling her that heaven was a beautiful place, and that her mother would be there someday to welcome her home. I guess everyone heard something different that night.

Ples played "The Two Sisters," "The Elfin Knight," and about a dozen more songs. When he stopped, the crowd came out of its trance, and everyone surged to their feet. They stomped and whooped, hollered, screamed, whistled, and hammered on the desks. It looked like the crowd was going to tear the schoolhouse down, so great was the excitement.

The crowd kept up its cheering while Judge Dunlap handed Ples the jug of whiskey and made a speech no one heard over the noise. Old Rob won the second place jug, which we'd provided just in case Ples made it to the contest. But no one noticed Old Rob. The crowd was still whistling and shouting and watching Ples, as he hooked a finger into the handle of the whiskey jug. Ples heisted the jug over his shoulder, jerked the corncob out of the mouth of the jug with his teeth, and took a long pull of whiskey—his Fiddler's Dram. Everyone cheered loudly.

And then Ples, the whiskey jug, and the fiddle all crashed to the floor. There was instant, stunned silence before everyone rushed to the stage. Judge Huley Dunlap made them stand back, shouting, "Get a doctor! I can't feel a heartbeat."

My girl gave a sob and clung to my arm. We all stared at Ples lying on the stage. None of us had noticed, while Ples was playing, that his clothes were covered with clay. Ples looked like he had walked through a swamp, and he was pale as death.

"Think of it," Mrs. Reddin said to Old Rob, "he came all the way to Dukedom to win the contest with his last breath."

"And it was the best I ever heard him play," said Old Rob. There was no envy in Old Rob. He liked Ples as much as the rest of us.

The doctor hurried in and knelt down to examine Ples.

"How did he get in here?" the doctor asked the judge.

"He walked in," said the judge, puzzled by the question. "He fiddled for a piece, and then keeled over dead before our eyes, poor man."

"Keeled over, my sainted granny!" the doctor exclaimed. "This man's been dead for at least forty-eight hours. And from the state of his clothes, I'd say he was buried too."

19

The Dead Chief

HIAWASSEE, GEORGIA

He knew it was wrong. Of course it was. He was desecrating an ancient grave on the bluff beside the river; a morally bankrupt idea by any people's standards. But Tom didn't care. The old native warrior had been dead for more than a hundred years. He wouldn't miss a few relics. Tom paused in his digging to brush sweat off his forehead and frowned when he heard the howl of a dog above the wind roaring down the river.

Tom had gotten this mad idea when some archeologists came to town to dig in the forest. They were looking for Native American relics to study, but so far they'd just come up with a few arrowheads. Tom was pretty sure they'd pay a lot of money for some real Native artifacts. And he knew where to get them. His Uncle Henry, who'd brought Tom up after his parents died, told the story of the finding of the bones each year on All Hallows Eve.

Many years ago, so the tale went, his uncle was walking the farm fence line near the river when he saw a skeleton partially buried in the bluff. The rain had washed the dirt away from the head and upper torso, and the hollow-eyed skull stared straight at Uncle Henry as if it recognized him. Uncle Henry was

THE DEAD CHIEF

spooked by the staring skeleton, but he still went to investigate his find. He uncovered enough of the skeleton to see that the corpse was wrapped with the fancy necklaces, arm bands and jewelry of a native chief. Uncle Henry fingered the relicts for a few minutes; then he decided to do the right thing and rebury the corpse with all the jewelry intact.

Shortly after he returned home, a fierce storm almost blew Uncle Henry's tiny cabin to pieces. He could distinctly hear native drum beating over the roar of the wind and rain. Uncle Henry knew that he'd stirred up the ghost of the chief with his disrespectful handling of the bones. Not knowing how else to placate the ghost, Uncle Henry went to the place on the bluff where the chief was buried and begged for forgiveness over and over until the storm dissipated into the night.

It was a great story to tell on All Hallows Eve, but Tom discounted the part about the ghost. He figured Uncle Henry was just trying to scare him so he wouldn't go looking for the warrior's skeleton. And this tactic had worked just fine when he was a little kid. But he turned fourteen on his last birthday, and he didn't believe in haunts no more. Tom pushed his shovel into the bluff and kept digging as the wind roared and the lone dog howled again in the fading afternoon light.

A moment later, Tom's shovel struck the first of the bones, and within five minutes he was staring into the knowing gaze of the chief's skull. Tom shivered, not liking the way that the skull seemed to follow his every move with the eyes it didn't have. Hastily, he stripped the skeleton of its arm bands and necklaces and amulets and other relicts. The archeologists would pay real well for this booty, Tom thought, pushing away his discomfort.

As he stripped a beaded decoration off a leg bone, Tom noticed that part of the skeleton's right foot was missing. So the chief had been crippled in life. Given the rich decorations with which he'd been buried, the injury obviously hadn't stopped him from achieving greatness.

Perhaps it was in overcoming his injury that he achieved greatness, a little voice murmured at the back of Tom's brain as the chief's skull eyed him knowingly.

Tom dropped the leg bone abruptly at the thought and stepped back from the corpse, goose-bumps prickling over his neck and arms. He shouldn't be doing this. This was wrong.

Somewhere behind the trees, the dog howled a third time; a mournful sound. Tom thrust the remaining jewelry into his bag and then quickly reburied the bones, starting with the smirking skull.

"I don't believe in haunts," Tom said aloud, shouldering the bag. A sudden wind barreled down the river, bending the tops of trees and knocking Tom sideways. He shuddered and raced for the old cabin he shared with Uncle Henry.

Tom left the bag of jewelry behind the woodpile where his uncle was unlikely to find it. He was certain that Uncle Henry would be angry with him for desecrating the chief's grave, and was determined that his uncle would never know about this day's work.

By the time Tom had washed off the dirt from his digging at the outside pump, thick clouds had rolled in. He barely reached the front door before heavy rain lashed the roof of the cabin.

"Ooo-eee, what a storm," Uncle Henry called, looking up from the frying pan where onions and potatoes sizzled. Tom sniffed the enticing smell, his mouth watering. He had worked up a mighty appetite with all that digging. "It reminds me of the night after I dug up that old chief's corpse," Uncle Henry continued, as if reading Tom's mind. "That storm nearly washed this old cabin away, it was so fierce."

Tom started guiltily. Why had Uncle Henry chosen tonight of all nights to mention the chief's skeleton?

The old man added some sausages to the skillet and stirred reminiscently. "I swear I saw the old chief out this very window," he gestured with the spoon. "He was standing there with his dog, waiting for me to apologize."

"His dog," asked Tom uneasily, a chill running up his spine as he remembered the dog that had howled three times while he dug up the skeleton.

Tom grabbed plates from the sideboard and started setting the table; avoiding his uncle's sharp eye. He was sure there was guilt plastered all over his face. "You never told me about a dog."

"I didn't? It was buried right beside the chief, guarding his master's crippled right foot," Uncle Henry said, beckoning for the plates. As he poured the contents of the frying pan into the dishes, he continued: "That's when I realized I had to rebury the chief, when I saw his faithful dog lying him in death as it must have done in life. It weren't right for me to disturb the pair."

"Oh," said Tom faintly as Uncle Henry took his place at the head of the table and said the blessing. Tom applied himself to eating so he could avoid his uncle's gaze as the storm slammed the cabin with mighty gusts of wind and the rain pounded so hard against the roof that it was a miracle it didn't pour through.

"Howdy man! Somebody's disturbed the elements tonight," Uncle Henry said, swallowing a last piece of sausage. "We'd best stay on our toes, boy. We may have to pack up quick and move to higher ground if this keeps up all night."

"Yes Uncle," Tom said, grabbing up the dishes and taking them to the sink. He poured warm water from the kettle on the stove into a pan and then did up the dishes while his uncle smoked a pipe before bed. Finally, Uncle Henry knocked the ashes out of his pipe and bade Tom goodnight.

When his uncle was safe inside the cabin's only bedroom, Tom sighed with relief. He'd be glad when the relicts were sold and he was done with this whole rotten business. Uncle Henry would be so pleased with the extra money he wouldn't be sore about the native chief's bones.

Pleased with this thought, Tom grabbed a candle and headed toward the ladder leading up to his bed in the loft. As he passed the window, he glanced out into the rain-lashed night and yipped in fright. Standing at the edge of the yard was the tall glowing figure of a Native American chief with a translucent dog at his side. Tom climbed up the ladder lickety-split, nearly dropping the candle and setting the cabin on fire. He ducked under the bedclothes and blew out the candle, praying the haunt would go away and leave him alone.

Tom's fear intensified with the darkness. Over and under and around the howl of the wind and the lash of the rain he could hear drums beating. Tom stuffed the pillow over his head, but the steady thump-thump-thumping vibrated through the walls and shook the bed.

"Go away, go away," he moaned into the mattress. But the drums didn't stop and the storm grew worse. The rain thundered so hard against the old cabin that it tore away a section of the roof and water hurled down on Tom's bed, soaking his blanket. An eerie glow filled the loft, as if the chief were gazing down at him through the gap in the roof.

Tom sat up with a scream of panic and tore off his blankets. "I'll give it back! I'll give it back right now!" He slid down the ladder without using the rungs and raced toward the door in his nightclothes. Uncle Henry appeared in the main room as Tom dragged on his boots and flung open the front door.

"Boy, don't go out in that storm! You'll be killed," he cried in alarm, fumbling to light the lantern.

"I gotta take it back and say I'm sorry," Tom wailed over the drumbeats. He could hear the dog howling and knew the chief was right outside.

Ignoring his uncle's panicked shout, he raced into the storm, stumbling as the icy rain struck his skin and mud sucked at his heavy boots. Tom staggered to the wood pile, grabbed the bag of jewelry and ran into the forest, heading for the river. Out of the corner of his eye, he saw the glowing figure limping after him, a translucent dog at its heels. He stumbled several times, nearly dropping the bag. Tree roots tripped him; his face was lashed by wind-blown branches; and blood poured from a cut over his left eye. He ran on, his feet keeping time to the beating of native drums. And always, the dead chief stalked a few yards behind him.

When Tom reached the bluff, the wind knocked him flat. He had to crawl through a river of mud to the place where the chief's skeleton lay buried. Clutching the bag between his knees so he wouldn't lose it in the darkness, Tom dug into the wet mud with his bare hands until the skull and bones were visible. Behind him, the dog howled chillingly as Tom fumbled to replaced the necklaces and arm bands and amulets and decorations. He winced when he saw the injured foot, and his shaking hands touched the smaller skull of the dog as he reburied the chief's bones in the desecrated grave. From somewhere behind him, the ghost dog howled.

"I'm sorry," Tom sobbed. "I'm sorry. I'm sorry! Your things are back just as they were. I put everything back."

He rolled over and screamed in terror, for the glowing chief and his dog were limping up the bluff just a few yards away. They were coming for him! And there was no place to hide.

Tom leapt to his feet and backed away from the glowing figures, his hands held up in front of his face to ward off whatever attack was coming. The chief drew closer and still closer until he was less than a yard away. He stretched out his hand toward the trembling boy. Beside him, the dog barked a warning. "I'm sorry," Tom screamed, stumbling back from the apparitions.

Suddenly, the ground fell away from his feet. Tom screamed in panic as his body plunged straight down toward the flooded river. His cry was broken off as he sank into the raging torrent. The current was unbelievably strong due to the terrible storm. The river swept Tom away; pulling his head down under the water. Severely hampered by his heavy night clothes and thick boots, Tom barely managed to fight his way to the surface and gasped for air. "I'm sorry. I'm sorry," Tom sobbed desperately. He was still apologizing as the current pulled him down to the bottom and smashed him against the stones. I'm sorry chief, he thought, his lungs red-hot with the terrible need to breathe. I deserve this death for desecrating your grave.

Just as Tom blacked out from lack of air, he felt a creature nudge up to his side and push him toward the bank. Then a strong pair of hands seized the back of his night clothes and pulled upward.

When Tom came back to his senses, it was dawn and the storm was over. Tom was lying several feet above the raging river on a muddy bank. He sat up blearily, wiping blood from his face and looked around for the person who'd saved him from the river. No one was there. But in the mud beside him, Tom saw two sets of footprints: one belonging to a dog and one belonging to a crippled man with half of a foot on the right side.

Tom gasped and nearly blacked out again. At that moment, he heard Uncle Henry call his name from the top of the bluff. Tom pushed himself into a sitting position and looked again at the footprints beside him. "Thank you," he whispered to the chief, tears rolling down his muddy cheeks. Then he stood up, legs wobbling, and waved up at his frantic uncle. With a shout of joy, Uncle Henry raced down to the river and hugged his shaking nephew with all his strength.

20

The Widow Jinks

On my second night home after mustering out from my company at the end of the Civil War, I woke up shivering in the sudden cold, wondering why the summer night felt so chilly. I rolled over and found myself looking at a glowing figure glaring at me from the foot of the bed. I was never so scared in my whole life. My body came all over with goose bumps and my hair positively stood on end. Gathering my courage, I exclaimed, "Who are you?"

"Name's Jinks," the specter said in a husky tone with an odd echo to it that made my flesh creep. "I'm the ghost of the rebel soldier you picked off in the battle of Bull Run."

My mind raced back to that fateful day. I'd picked off more than one rebel during that horror on the battlefield. Which one was this? Then I had it. "Are you the chap that hid behind the old log? The one that kept ducking down whenever I took aim? I didn't think I hit you."

"You sure did, seeing as I've been a ghost ever since that day," the specter growled. "I'm here to demand reparation."

THE WIDOW JINKS

"Reparation?" I said indignantly, sitting up and hugging my knees to my chest. "What do you mean, reparation? We faced off in a battle. It was a fair fight. I can't bring you back to life."

"You can't," Jinks said in sepulchral tones. "But there's my widow to consider. I looked in on her yesterday and she's having a hard time getting along. You must hunt her up and tell her to dig the little farm for coal."

My ears perked up. Coal? There was good money to be had in coal. "How do you know there's coal there?" I asked skeptically.

The glowing figure gave an eerie smile. "It is my province to know things denied to you mortals. Now, will you go?"

I considered thoughtfully. I didn't much like my current job, and a potentially rich widow sounded mighty tempting. I loved my mother, but once a fellow has been living on his own, he really prefers his own place. "Where is your widow living now?" I asked.

"It's not far," said the ghost of Mr. Jinks. He gave very specific directions to a place in Maryland. I listened intently and started calculating the cost of taking such a trip. A high sum.

"When can you start?" growled the specter.

"I'll head south tomorrow. I should see your widow in about ten days," I replied. "Do you have a message you wish to send?"

Jinks sat himself down on the bed—or tried too. He sank too deeply into the mattress. "No message," he said emphatically. "As a ghost, I can only appear to the person who caused my death. If I send a message to Melinda through you, she'll know you killed me, and boy howdy will you get it. Still, I thought lots of her, and she just worshiped me, even when we didn't agree." He gave a gusty sigh that made the hairs on my neck prickle.

How interesting. So Jinks and his wife didn't get along when he was still in the land of the living. "Why didn't you agree?" I asked curiously.

"Melinda was very industrious," Jinks said. "She was always working. And I was born tired. She never understood that. Come to think of it, you may have done me a good turn at Bull Run. Now I don't have to hustle for anything to eat, the heat doesn't bother me, and I can rest whenever I like. When Melinda is provided for, I promise I'll stop haunting you. Just keep it a dead secret that you killed me. Melinda loved me to desperation despite everything, and if she knew you done me in, she'd kill you and send your ghost a-wandering like mine."

"I'll make sure your widow is provided for," I said vaguely. "And I accept your promise to stop haunting me when I do."

Jinks nodded several times and then spiraled away until the room was dark once more.

I left promptly the next morning and made my way slowly south. I'd recently taken on the job of selling patent washing machines, and my new employers didn't care where I sold them, so when I told them I was heading to Maryland, they wished me a good journey and that was that. So I worked my way south with my merchandise, heading toward poor, lonely Widow Jinks—and the coal in her backyard.

During my journey south, if the householders permitted it, I would bring the washing machine inside and wash a few pieces of their linen to show them how it worked. We shared tips on the best methods of stain removal and how to get a collar good and stiff. I became quite an expert in the art of washing.

All of this was good practice for my encounter with Widow Jinks. My plan was to ask Mrs. Jinks to board at her place while I sold my washers to the folks in the surrounding county, and I'd ingratiate myself by helping her with the laundry on washday. I figured I had to feel my way carefully before mentioning a possible coalfield. Otherwise, she'd call me a scallywag and send me packing.

Exactly ten days later, I reached the Jinks place in Allegany County, Maryland. I knocked on the door, and it was opened by an old woman. My heart plummeted. I'd been expecting a young lady. The ghost of Mr. Jinks hadn't looked old. But apparently I'd assumed wrong. Still, I'd given my word to the specter that I'd help his widow, so I would stick with the plan.

"Is this Mrs. Jinks?" I asked politely.

"Law, no," the old lady smiled. "I'm Mrs. Friedman who lives with her now that her no-good husband has passed. Step inside and rest a bit while we wait for Melinda. She's running some errands and should be along shortly."

The front room was neat and clean, but there wasn't much furniture. The pieces were rather threadbare and worn, just as I expected from what the ghost of Jinks told me. Mrs. Friedman and I hit it off splendidly. She quickly confided to me that Melinda Jinks was far better off without her husband, who she described as the most shiftless and lazy man that ever lived.

Mrs. Friedman broke off suddenly and gestured toward the window. "Here comes Melinda now," she said with a fond smile. I gazed through the glass at a lovely dark-haired woman with bright eyes and a resolute chin. She looked like she wouldn't take any nonsense from a lazy husband, and I liked her the better for it. In fact, I was pretty taken with the Widow Jinks right from the start. She listened intently to Mrs. Friedman's introduction, and her attention sharpened further when I said, "I had the honor of being connected with the late Mr. Jinks during the war. It was his earnest desire, if he was killed, that I should carry a message of his undying affection for you. It has been impossible for me to reach you until now, but please rest assured I came as quickly as I could."

"Thank you very much for your kindness, Mr. Wilkins," Widow Jinks said. "I am glad to meet someone who knew William during the war."

I winced inwardly at her kind words and felt like a fraud. Still, this was what the ghost of Jinks wanted me to do.

Oddly, she did not ask for further particulars about her husband, and I didn't pursue the matter. Instead, I described the business that brought me to this part of the country and asked if she would be willing to board me while I worked. Widow Jinks said she'd take me in, and though she didn't say so, I received the impression that she and Mrs. Friedman were glad of the extra income.

On my first night at the cottage, I again had a spectral visitor. Mr. Jinks appeared at the foot of my bed in his Confederate uniform. I rubbed my eyes sleepily and growled, "What now? I'm here like you asked me to be. Can't you let me sleep in peace?"

"I just wanted to know how you are coming on," the ghost grumbled.

"Well enough so far," I said, sitting up with a sigh. "But it's going to be a slow business breaking the news of the coalfield to her."

"Why is that?" asked William Jinks suspiciously.

"Because she's got to have faith in me, or she'll think I'm telling tall tales," I replied. "If she doesn't believe me, she won't go looking for the coal and your haunting will be in vain."

The specter was much struck by my words. "That's true. Melinda is no pushover. Still, you should hurry it up as fast as you can. Melinda hates to have a man bothering about the place." With that piece of advice, the ghost vanished.

Well, she certainly didn't care to have you hanging about, I thought as I rolled over and went back to sleep.

The next few weeks were the happiest I'd ever lived. I had wonderful luck selling my patent washing machines. When I wasn't meeting friendly people and making their lives a little bit better, I was doing odd jobs around the house to earn my keep. My mother taught me to make myself useful and that's just what I did. I repaired the fence, fixed the leaking roof, built a shed, chopped firewood, and fixed Mrs. Friedman's spinning wheel. And so forth.

In the evenings, I'd sit with the ladies on the little front porch and tell them lighthearted stories from my days as a soldier. We laughed heartily at some of the antics the men got up to between battles. Widow Jinks and Mrs. Friedman countered with little stories about the people and animals living in the region, and their tales were equally interesting to me.

The disclosure of the coalfield had completely slipped my mind until a month to the day after my arrival, when the ghost of Mr. Jinks appeared once again in my room.

"What is the meaning of this delay?" the specter demanded. He was so angry that blue sparks shot out of his glowing body in all directions.

"Relax, Jinks," I said uneasily. The ghost was quite disconcerting. For the first time, I wondered if Jinks would harm me if I didn't obey his request. "I am going to tell her tomorrow."

"See that you do," the ghost said with a red-eyed glare. "Or I'll run you off the place."

"Hogwash," I said.

I decided the ghost was more bluster than business. Still, I'd given my word. It was time to act. And once my part of the bargain was fulfilled, the ghost couldn't haunt me anymore. Jinks had given me his promise.

The next evening, I found Widow Jinks alone on the porch. "Mrs. Friedman has gone to the village," she explained.

"I'm glad I caught you alone," I said, sitting down on the steps at her feet. "I've been wishing to tell you something. I've made a discovery while working around your place, and it's something I can tell only to you."

Mrs. Jinks clasped her hands tightly together, and I felt her gaze on me. Her eyes were dark and luminous in the moonlight.

"I think there is coal on this land, right underneath your house," I said, addressing the stick in my hand instead of the lovely woman beside me. "If this is true, you stand to become a wealthy woman. If you don't have the means to make the investigation yourself, I am happy to advance you whatever capital you need as a partial share in the mine, should coal be found." I reddened and added, "You wouldn't have to pay me back if it's a false alarm. It's just what anyone speculating on coal would do in my place."

Melinda Jinks straightened herself, and it seemed as if she was disappointed somehow. I turned to look at her. "How do you know there is coal here?" she asked. Her voice was cool, and I'd never heard that tone from her before. My heart sank.

"Your husband told me his suspicions about it. I wanted to make sure his idea was correct before telling you. I didn't want to raise false hopes," I explained.

"You are very kind," the Widow Jinks said, still in that cool tone. "I'll go in now and think it over."

She rose, and it felt like a wall had been erected between us. I was devastated. I reached out suddenly and caught her hand. She paused and looked down at me.

"I've discovered something else," I said in a husky voice. "But I am afraid to tell you."

Melinda Jinks slowly sank down into her chair. Her eyes were suddenly warm, and my heart started to pound against my ribs. She didn't speak, but I could tell she wanted me to continue.

"I've discovered that you are the one woman in the world for me," I said. "But how can I ask you to marry me when you will be rich and I am just a poor soldier who sells washing machines?"

Melinda's eyes told me what she thought of that nonsense.

"Will you have me?" I asked humbly.

She smiled, and I knelt on the top step and took her in my arms.

"We don't have to do anything about the coalfield," I told her after our first kiss. "I'll take you to meet my family, and then we can settle anywhere you like. I can earn a good living selling washing machines."

"Pshaw," said my lady. "Why would we ignore the coalfield? It will be money for our children and grandchildren."

"And Mrs. Friedman will live with us. She'll like having children underfoot," I continued. "I suggest we have a new house built in the town while I take you to meet my family. After that, if you wish, we can begin work on the coalfield."

Melinda gave me another kiss to confirm our plan.

"I confess I feel much better now that you know about the coal," I said. "I feel like Mr. Jinks can rest in peace now that you are taken care of."

"Mr. Jinks," Melinda said crisply, "was always very good at resting. You, on the other hand, are very good at working. Which is why I will have you or none."

This declaration earned her a third kiss.

I waited several hours after I retired for the ghost to arrive. Jinks swirled into being in a flash of blue light at the foot of my bed and eyed me expectantly. "Did you tell her?" he demanded eagerly.

"I told her," I confirmed. "She is very happy."

The ghost of Mr. Jinks rubbed his hands with glee. "That's good, that's good," he cried. "I'm obliged to you for your trouble, though frankly I don't see how you could have done much less. Still, a promise is a promise. I'll stop haunting you now. You are free to go back north."

"And what are you going to do?" I asked, curious about how a ghost occupied itself once its earthly mission was complete.

"Me? I'll keep Melinda company from now on," said William Jinks. "She won't be able to see me, of course, but I'm sure it will gladden her lonely heart to feel my presence in this house. Now, how soon can you leave? I don't wish to be inhospitable, but this house is mine and I've decided to live here permanently. The sooner you get away, the better."

I was nettled by his obvious desire to be rid of me. After all, I'd done him a favor. "I am going as soon as I can get married," I told him. "In about two days' time."

"Married?" said the ghost. "Well, well. So, you found yourself a bride during your stay here! I only hope that you get as devoted a wife as my Melinda."

"I am quite sure I have," I said briskly. "And my bride and I will be happy to leave you in possession of these premises."

William Jinks eyed me suspiciously. "Who'd you say you were going to marry?" he asked.

"Melinda Jinks," I said.

The ghost of Mr. Jinks reared up in shock and started sparking blue flames from every part of his body. He was furious, and I could tell he wanted to kill me right there and then. But he'd promised to stop haunting me if I did as he bade me, and I knew he couldn't touch me. The flaming ghost lunged toward me, arms outstretched to grab and strangle. I held my ground, certain that I was right. Just before Jinks reached me, he hit a wall of pure white energy that flung him backward with such force that he vanished through the far wall.

"Good riddance," I said in satisfaction.

And that was the last time I saw the ghost of Mr. Jinks.

21

Beelzebub

About two years ago, by my reckoning, the whole town was swept by ghost hysteria. Sammy Stonestreet burst into the inn at a dead run one night and got himself roaring drunk before he was able to describe a ghost he saw among the tombstones. "It was crying and talking to itself," he gasped, taking a deep swig from his mug. "It wandered about like a lost soul, poor thing. It scared the wits out of me, bleating like a little lamb!"

The story made monstrous talk for more than ten miles around the settlement. Everyone had a theory about who the ghost might be. The most popular explanation was that old Mr. Walker, who died a pauper, might be seeking his revenge against the lawyers who stole all his property. But no one could be sure.

Sammy was the first of many who encountered the local haunt. Bob Moreland saw it wandering aimlessly among the graves on his way to visit his betrothed. Later that week, Missus Carol nearly died of fright when the ghost sneezed as it meandered past her wagon. "It cried in agony as it fled through the cemetery gates," she told her daughter, fanning herself vigorously with her handkerchief.

BEELZEBUB

By this time, half the town wouldn't leave their homes after dark. Those brave enough to venture out at night avoided the cemetery road, sometimes going twice the length of their actual journey to avoid the haunt. A few of the "bad boys" in town boasted that they were going to spend the night in the cemetery with the ghost, but somehow they never got around to it.

The identity of the ghost might have gone completely unknown if Bill Wilson hadn't come to town to visit his old nanna. He was a brave chap, by all accounts, and didn't believe in ghosts. So when the talk turned to the local haunt one night down at the tavern, Bill scoffed at everyone for believing in nonsense.

"Nonsense, you say?" asked Mr. Harley, who owned the place. "Five dollars says you won't go into the graveyard alone after dark."

"Put up your stakes," Bill Wilson said. "I ain't afraid of a ghost. In fact, if you lend me those pistols of yours and a bottle of whiskey to keep me company, I'll stay the whole night and prove to you that there's no such thing as haunts!"

"Done," Mr. Harley said at once.

Bill Wilson downed a couple more drinks for courage, then belted on the loaned pistols and swaggered out the door with bottle in hand. Mr. Harley and the other gamblers trailed him down the road in the twilight, wondering what he intended to do.

"Is it possible to shoot a ghost?" Henry Jasper asked the blacksmith.

"Dunno. Guess we'll find out," the blacksmith replied.

When Bill Wilson reached the gates of the graveyard, everyone else veered off and watched from the far side of the road as he paused by the high post-and-rail fence.

"You watch out for yourself, Bill Wilson," called Henry Jasper. "Those ghosts is monstrous, dangerous things."

"Never you mind about them," Bill swaggered. "Just remember, I aim to shoot any haunts I see!"

"Yessir," the crowd chorused.

The gamblers watched in horrified fascination as Bill marched straight through the big lot full of moldering tombstones and settled himself at the foot of a grave topped by a weeping angel that sat dead center in the cemetery. On the far side of the graveyard, the pine forest whispered in the evening breeze. The hissing of the pine fronds made more than one chap shudder and turn away. As the group dispersed, Bill took a swig from his whiskey bottle and started singing hymns to keep himself awake.

The night grew colder and darker. Little rustles and soft clicks that went unheeded during the day resounded like gunshots in the silence of the cemetery, causing Bill to twitch more than once. The wind whistled and hissed and ran icy fingers down his neck. Bill kept on drinking and singing, trying to ignore it all. One of the pistols lay cocked in his lap in case something came running at him from among the gravestones. It was so dark that he couldn't see more than ten feet around him. The creak and moan of the breeze in the branches and the hiss and sway of the leaves against the darkness of the cloudy sky made his hair stand on end. He thought about backing out of the deal, but a bet is a bet. He took another swig of whiskey, which steadied his nerves but made him sleepy. So very sleepy. Bill felt his head nodding toward his chest, and there wasn't anything he could do about it.

Something sneezed just a few feet from his seat under the weeping angel.

"What's that?" shouted Bill, jerked out of his doze.

He searched the surrounding darkness, every nerve alert, but there was no misty figure, no white light. Nothing but a hissing wind in the trees. Even the soft rustle of night creatures had stilled.

Bill decided he must have sneezed in his sleep. He relaxed and took a large swig of whiskey. Then he checked to make sure the pistol was ready in case any more sneezing haunts came his way and settled back to sleep. Only a few paces away, several white figures drifted into the graveyard through a gap in the fence near the pine woods.

Bill was awakened a second time when a smelly white spirit started sniffing his privates. Then it thrust its heinous whiskery essence into his face and gave a piteous bleat of despair.

"Wha . . . Gerroff . . . oh my lordy in heaven," Bill gasped as his eyes finally opened and he found himself gazing into a horrible white face with eyes as dark as the grave and devil's horns on its head.

The haunt was offended by this appeal to the Almighty, for it took a step back, lowered its devil's horns, and smashed Bill in the face. Bill's cranium ricocheted off the gravestone and his body slithered sideways, landing in a heap on the grass. The pistol went off with an enormous bang, and the weeping angel, loosened from many years of storms and erosion, toppled onto Bill's head.

"Murder," Bill screamed, fighting furiously with his winged attacker. "Murder!"

Mr. Harley and his fellow gamblers burst forth from their bedchambers and came running to the graveyard to see what kind of haunt had got hold of poor Bill Wilson. They found him wrestling with a stone angel, his broken nose knocked flat as a pancake and both eyes so bruised and swollen that he could hardly tell lantern light from dark.

"Them haunts tried to kill me," Bill shouted at the group. "Their leader was a demon that was ten feet tall with devil's horns atop its head! It tried to steal my soul, but I whupped it good and proper. When I aimed my pistol, it threw a lightning bolt at my face and a thunderclap knocked me clean over. Then a second ghost jumped me from behind! But I managed to wrestle that one to the ground, as you can see here."

Everyone looked from the toppled statue to the milling herd of goats quietly munching their way through the cemetery's flower arrangements. Bill Wilson beamed at his fellow gamblers, peering into their faces through his goat-blackened eyes. Henry Jasper clapped a hand over his mouth to keep from snickering aloud as he realized just who—or what—had been haunting the cemetery. A murmur of astonished revelation ran through the rest of the group, but before anyone could blurt out the truth, the blacksmith waved them to silence. Poor, bruised Bill Wilson was so proud of himself for facing down the horrible haunt that no one wanted to disabuse him of his heroic act.

"Well Bill, you took on old Beelzebub himself and lived to tell the tale," Mr. Harley said gravely, staring at the defiant billy goat, which was chomping on a wreath of roses. Old Beelzebub shook his horns at the innkeeper, daring him to take away his meal. "You earned your five dollars, sure enough."

Mr. Harley helped the ghost buster out of the cemetery and made sure he was tucked up safely in his nanna's cottage, then went to meet his fellow gamblers on the porch of the inn. As soon as he arrived, the whole group burst out laughing and didn't stop until Mrs. Harley opened the parlor window and threatened to pour a bucket of water over the lot of them if they didn't hush.

Bill Wilson's ghost story was the talk of the settlement the next morning. The gamblers egged on the ghost buster with sly smiles, and his tale grew more elaborate with each repetition. While Bill reveled in his heroics, Mr. Harley and the blacksmith went quietly over to the cemetery to replace the angel on top of its tombstone and mend the back fence.

Thwarted of access to his strange new pasture, old Beelzebub, leader of the local goat herd, led his fair maidens to a new meadow on the far side of the pine wood. And that put an end to the nightly ghost sightings in the local cemetery.

22

The Black Umbrella

MOUNT PLEASANT, SOUTH CAROLINA

They say that the dead never forget the dead. And old Mary Simmons can tell you that's true. Every year in the spring, just before Easter, the departed saints rise from their graves and hold a remembrance service for the forgotten dead who perished alone during the past year. At least, that's how the old story goes.

Mary was working as a cook in those days. She lived in a small cottage in an old neighborhood, right next to a tiny charitable cemetery where the poor and forgotten were buried.

The little graveyard was almost as neglected as the folks who lay in it. Mary sometimes put flowers on the graves because she thought somebody should care. She also cleared the worst of the weeds out of the cemetery each month, out of respect for the dead. But she was the only one to visit the tiny burying ground.

One drizzly Sunday afternoon, Mary was dozing in the comfortable seat by her window when she was awakened by the sound of chanting coming from the old burying ground.

"No more rain is going to wet you, no more. Oh, Lord, I want to go home."

THE BLACK UMBRELLA

Mary snapped awake, recognizing the old chant for the dead that they used during funeral processions when she was a child. Were they coming to bury some poor, forgotten soul that passed away? She'd appointed herself the keeper of this old burying place. The least she could do was honor the fallen one with her beautiful singing voice.

Mary put on her hat and slipped out into the rain. She hurried next door and saw a group of mourners gathered in the center of the graveyard. Mary joined the mourners and sang with all her heart: "No more cold is going to cold you, no more. Oh, Lord, I want to go home."

The heavens opened above them as they sang in the growing dusk, and the rain came pouring down in heavy sheets. A cold wind whipped around them and blew Mary's hat away. But the singing continued.

A tall man in a black coat caught Mary's hat and returned it to her. "Sister," he said. "A song like yours needs a good cover." He pushed the handle of his big black umbrella into her hands and ducked away into the crowd before she could give it back.

So Mary kept on singing with all her heart, tears mingling with the raindrops on her cheeks. "No more rain is going to wet you, no more. No more cold is going to cold you, no more. Oh, Lord, I want to go home."

When the chant ceased, she heard the voice of the preacher deep within the crowd of saints praying over the departed souls. Mary bowed her head and prayed with him.

"The blessing of the Almighty God who hears the cries of the poor be upon you now and forevermore," the preacher intoned at the close of his prayer. "Amen."

All the mourners responded: "Amen!"

The word reverberated around Mary like a clap of thunder. It shook the very ground on which she stood. The sound seemed to stretch into the vastness of eternity, as if every saint from every age repeated it with the mourners.

When Mary lifted her head, she was shocked to find that she was standing alone in the small, forsaken graveyard. No footprints marred the surface of the overgrown grass. No flowers were strewn over the graves. It was clear that no one had set foot in this place for years, except for herself. All the mourners had vanished, as if they were . . .

Mary swallowed, not wanting to complete the thought.

As if they were ghosts, a stubborn little voice whispered insistently in her mind.

Frightened, Mary hurried home in the pouring rain, stumbling over the unkempt lawn and nearly tripping on the doorstep of her home. It was only when she was fumbling with the knob of the front door that she realized she was still holding the big black umbrella that the tall man had given her.

She gasped and almost dropped it. The umbrella was real, so surely the man who had given it to her was real. Wasn't he?

Mary looked back toward the burying ground, searching the rain-streaked twilight for a glimpse of the tall man. No one was there. The road beside the cemetery was empty and still. The only sound was the rain hissing as it hit the surface of the puddles and agitated the leaves of the trees. A wind whisked around her questioningly. Why was she standing out in the cold?

Shivering, Mary hurried into the house and closed the door. She shook the umbrella dry and then set it carefully in the corner, wondering if the ghost of the tall man would stop by and ask for it back. If he did, would she be brave enough to open the door and return it? She wasn't sure. But one thing she did know. She would never follow another unknown funeral procession. She would find another way to honor the forgotten dead.

PART TWO
The Powers of Darkness

23

The Wampus Cat

KNOXVILLE, TENNESSEE

The missus and me, we were just setting down to a late-night piece of apple pie when we heard someone running real fast across our barnyard.

"Casper! Casper!" a man was shouting. I recognized the voice of our new neighbor, Jeb Thomas. I swung the door open, and he ran inside looking as if he thought the devil were after him.

"Shut the door!" shouted Jeb. "Shut it quick!"

I shut the door and my missus tried to calm Jeb down a bit. Just then we heard a terrible howling coming from the barnyard. Jeb nearly fainted at the sound, and the dogs started whining by the fire. I could hear the other animals out in the barn squawking and mooing and neighing their distress at the terrible howling sound.

I knew at once what was making that sound. It was the Wampus cat. I took down my Bible and started reading Psalm 23 in a loud voice. I knew the Wampus cat couldn't stand the words of the Bible, no sir.

The Wampus cat let out one more piercing howl and then I heard it crashing back through the trees, away from the house.

THE WAMPUS CAT

I read a few more psalms just to be safe, then put the Bible back on the shelf and went to help my missus get Jeb into a chair. She gave him some hot coffee and cut him a slice of apple pie. Once Jeb had some pie in him, he was ready to tell us what happened.

"I was out late hunting with my dogs," Jeb began, eyeing his empty plate wistfully. "I could hear something howling out in the woods nearby, but I thought it was just wolves, and the dogs didn't seem to mind it. The dogs got way ahead of me. I kept calling them, but they didn't come back.

"I was trying to decide if I should keep looking for the dogs or just go home when I tripped over a root and fell. My rifle went flying somewhere. As I groped around for it, I smelled this awful smell. It smelled like one of my dogs had fallen into a bog after it messed with a skunk. I called the dogs again, expecting to see Rex or Sam come running up from wherever they'd gotten to. But when I looked up, I saw a pair of big yellow eyes glowing down at me, and there were these huge fangs dripping with saliva. The creature looked kind of like a mountain lion, but it was walking upright like a person. Then it howled, and I thought my skin would turn inside out. I got up and ran as fast as I could, that creature chasing me all the way. Sometimes it was so close I could feel its breath on my neck! I figured your house was closer than mine, so that's why I came here."

Jeb mopped his brow with his sleeve. He was sweating again at the memory, and his hands were shaking. The missus cut him another slice of pie and poured some more coffee.

"I never saw anything like it, Casper," Jeb said after consoling himself with a few bites of pie. "What in the world was that thing and how did you get rid of it? And do you think it got my dogs?"

"That was the Wampus cat," said my missus before I could finish swallowing my coffee. "They say that the Wampus cat used to be a beautiful Indian woman. The men of her tribe were always going on hunting trips, but the women had to stay home. The Indian woman secretly followed her husband one day when he went hunting with the other men. She hid herself behind a rock, clutching the hide of a mountain cat around her, and spied on the men as they sat around their campfires telling sacred stories and doing magic. According to the laws of the tribe, it was absolutely forbidden for women to hear the sacred stories and see the tribe's magic. So when the Indian woman was discovered, the medicine man punished her by binding her into the mountain cat skin she wore and transforming her into the creature you saw—half woman and half mountain cat. She is doomed forever to roam the hills, howling desolately because she wants to return to her normal body. They say she eats farm animals and even some young children."

"Well now," I said when my missus had finished her story, "that's one version of the tale. But myself, I think the truth lies in another direction."

I took another swallow of coffee. Jeb waved his fork impatiently and said, "Go on, Casper."

"Not so long ago, an old woman moved into a small house way back up in the hills near here. She lived like a hermit, and acted real unfriendly when the folks hereabouts tried to be neighborly. She was a strange woman, with wild hair and a crooked nose and a way of looking at you like she was reading your mind. It wasn't long before the folks around here starting calling her a witch because of the way the cattle and sheep acted after she came. Sometimes the cattle would fall over for no reason at all and lay like they were dead. Or the sheep would walk around in circles till they fell down. Some animals rammed themselves to death against barn walls. It was like someone had hexed the farms in these parts.

"Then animals started going missing, and people really got stirred up. We began hearing rumors about a strange black cat that could sometimes be seen in the barnyards around the county. Folks said the cat was really the witch. People claimed that the witch, disguised as a cat, would sneak into a farmhouse during the day when the door was open. The witch would hide herself somewhere in the house until the family went to bed at night, and then she would put a spell on the family so no one would wake before morning. Once her spell was completed, the witch would go to the barn and steal whatever animal she fancied. No one had ever caught the witch stealing an animal, but everyone knew that she was the one to blame.

"Finally, the townsfolk decided to lay a trap for the witch. One of the farmers had just gotten a fine new ram, which he had seen the witch looking over real carefully one day when the herd was out grazing. The farmer was sure the witch would try to steal the ram, so they set the trap at his house.

"Sure enough, that night the witch snuck into the house in her cat form and put the whole family under her spell. Then she jumped out the window and went to the barn to get the farmer's new ram. Once she was safely in the barn, the witch began to chant the spell to turn herself back into a human. Before she could finish the spell, several men jumped out and captured her. The witch was halfway through her spell when the trap was sprung, and she didn't have a chance to complete the transformation. She had grown to the size of a woman and was standing upright, but much of her was still a cat, including her large yellow eyes and the fangs. The half-woman half-cat creature was a terrible sight. Because the witch had been interrupted at a critical juncture, the spell could not be completed or reversed. The witch was trapped in this ghastly form forever.

"The witch howled in terror and struggled to free herself from her captors. She was strong as an ox in the new, misshapen form, and she knocked the men to the barn floor. Then she fled, breaking through the closed barn door in her haste, and disappeared into the hills.

"There was no more hexing of the farm animals after that, but the witch still walks the hills hereabouts, and still stalks farm animals when she can. Folks started calling her the Wampus cat, and they stay indoors on nights when the moon is high and the wind blows strong."

"Nights like tonight," Jeb said thoughtfully, pushing aside his coffee cup. "You never said how you got rid of the Wampus cat."

"Like all witches, the Wampus cat can't stand the sound of Scripture being read," I replied.

"Do you reckon it's safe to go home?" Jeb asked. "My missus will be worrying. And I'd like to see if Rex and Sam made it back."

"I'll drive you home," I said. "We'll take my dogs and the lanterns."

"And your Bible," Jeb said quickly.

"And my Bible," I agreed.

"Well," Jeb said as I got my coat. "I wouldn't have believed in that Wampus cat unless I'd seen it for myself. But I believe in it now!"

Jeb wished my missus goodnight and followed me out into the barnyard, glancing nervously into the nearby woods and clutching my Bible as he walked. Jeb helped hitch my horse up to the wagon, and before we left the barnyard, we lit the lanterns and put the dogs in the back.

As we traveled the short distance to Jeb's place, we could hear the Wampus cat howling in the distance. And closer, we could hear Jeb's dogs howling from his yard. Jeb sagged with relief. When we drove into the yard, Sam and Rex came to greet us. After fussing over his dogs for a bit, Jeb turned to me and said, "Thanks, Casper, for coming to my rescue."

I was just turning the wagon when Jeb opened the front door and called out, "I tell you one thing, Casper. I'm never going hunting at night again!" Then he slammed the door shut, and the dogs and I headed for home.

24

The Man in Gold

GUILFORD COUNTY, NORTH CAROLINA

There was once a very proud girl who lived in a huge mansion not too far from Guilford County. Her father doted upon his daughter and indulged her whenever he could. When she stated that she was not going to marry any man unless he came to her dressed all in gold, her father made no objection. The girl's little brother, who was very wise, told her that she would live to regret her rash words. But the daughter just laughed at him.

One evening, the father and mother gave a fancy ball for their daughter. Everyone who was anyone attended. The daughter danced and laughed and flirted with all the young men. But none of them caught her fancy.

Her little brother, bored with the party, went down to the gate to talk with the coachmen. While he was there, a fancy carriage driven by a hooded, featureless man and pulled by four fine black horses stopped at the gate. A handsome man, dressed all in gold, stepped out of the carriage.

"I am here to see the man of the house on business," the elegant man said to the gatekeeper. The little brother watched the man from behind the gate. There was something not quite right about the man in gold, but he could not put his finger on

THE MAN IN GOLD

what was wrong. The gatekeeper, awed by the fancy carriage, the fine black horses, and the gold clothing, let the man in at once.

As the man entered the courtyard, the little brother bowed to him and said, "I will take you to my father."

The father was pleased to meet the elegant man dressed in gold.

"It seems I have interrupted a ball," the man in gold said after they had been introduced. "I could come back at another time."

"Oh no, sir. Please join us. My daughter would like to meet you," said the father.

Indeed, the daughter was thrilled to meet the handsome man dressed in gold. She abandoned all the other young men and would dance with no one else the rest of the evening. The little brother stayed in the ballroom, studying the elegant man partnering his sister. Something was not quite right about the man. Then the little brother noticed that the elegant man's boots were too small for his size, as if his legs ended in something other than feet. Yet he danced with grace and skill.

Between dance sets, the little brother said to his sister, "Sister, did you notice the man's feet?"

"What about his feet?" asked the daughter lazily, waving her fan and watching the man in gold pouring her a drink of lemonade.

"His boots are too small and yet he dances as if his feet were normal. You should ask him about it."

"Ask him yourself," said the daughter as her escort came back with her drink.

"What is it you wish to ask me?" inquired the man in gold.

"What is wrong with your feet?" asked the little brother.

The elegant man raised an eyebrow, then frowned as if he thought the boy's question impertinent. But he answered it. "When I was a child, I fell into the fire and my feet were partially burned off. Fortunately, I overcame my handicap."

The man in gold bowed to the daughter and swept her onto the dance floor. The little brother frowned. It seemed to him that there was still something wrong. He studied the man in gold intently. The man's hands looked rather strange. They were gnarled and red, with very long nails that looked like claws. When the man and the sister returned to their chairs for a short rest, the brother said to the man, "Did you burn your hands too?"

"Really, brother!" His sister was annoyed. "That is rude. Apologize immediately."

The little brother apologized, and the man in gold graciously accepted his apology. But the man's eyes were cold, and the little brother felt it was prudent to leave the couple alone.

By the end of the ball, the man in gold and the daughter of the house were betrothed. The man, impatient to claim his bride, told the parents that he would take her to his home where they would be married. The parents were dazzled by the man's obvious wealth and agreed to let their daughter go away with him. The daughter, though completely infatuated by the man in gold, was a bit nervous about marrying in such haste.

"I will go with you gladly, sir," she said. "But I am going to a strange place and wish to have someone from my family accompany me. Little brother, will you come?"

The little brother agreed at once. He did not like the man in gold, and did not want his sister to marry the man. The man had his carriage brought around, and he settled his bride-to-be and her brother inside. The little brother looked out the window and saw the man in gold toss an egg into the air. It transformed into a large bird.

"Hop and skip, Betty. Go along and prepare the road for us," the man said.

The large bird flew away. The man stepped into the carriage, and the featureless coachman drove them out the gate and down the road in the direction the large bird had flown. The man in gold was silent, gazing out at the dark night. The daughter took her little brother's hand. Her fingers were shaking. The little brother squeezed his sister's hand and looked carefully around the carriage, seeking something to aid them should they need it. He saw a grubby sack underneath the seat across from them, where the man in gold sat. Otherwise, the carriage was empty.

Ahead of the carriage, a glow appeared on the horizon. It grew brighter and brighter as the carriage drove toward it. Smoke filled the air and blew into the carriage. The daughter and her brother started coughing.

"Sir, we cannot go that way. There is a fire," said the daughter.

"That is just my men burning off new ground for my crops," the man in gold said impatiently.

"Please sir, we cannot breathe through this smoke. We must turn aside," said the daughter. She was very nervous now. The man in gold was looking less and less like a handsome man the closer they got to the fire.

"I will check to see if there is a clear passage," the man in gold said. He asked the coachman to stop, swept up the grubby sack, and stepped out of the carriage.

The little brother saw him take an egg out of the sack and throw it up in the air. It transformed into a large bird.

"Hop and skip, Betty," the man said. "Clear the smoke for our passage home."

He stood watching as the large bird flew toward the fire.

"Brother, I am scared," said the daughter as they watched the man out the window.

"Sister, you should be scared. That is no man. That is the devil."

The little brother reached under the opposite seat, searching for something he could use against the man in gold. He found an egg that had rolled out of the grubby sack.

"Come sister," said the little brother. He pulled his sister out the door on the far side of the carriage. Then the little brother threw the egg into the air. The egg transformed into a large bird.

"Hop and skip, Betty," said the little brother. "Carry us home."

At once the huge bird picked them up in its claws and flew the brother and sister back to their parents' home.

The daughter was very glad to be back home. She wept and told her parents the whole story. They were grateful that their children had escaped. But the little brother was not so sure they had escaped. While the parents led their daughter to her bed to rest, her brother slipped down to the village to talk to May Brown, the local wisewoman.

After May Brown heard the little brother's tale, she nodded her head. "That bird will fly right back to the devil, and the devil will know your sister has returned to her home. The devil will come for her since she is promised to him in marriage."

"What should we do then?" asked the little brother.

"I will engage the devil in a riddle contest," said the wisewoman. "If I win, then the devil will leave your sister alone. If I lose, then she will have to marry him and go to live with him in General Cling Town."

"What's General Cling Town?" asked the little brother.

"General Cling Town is what we wisewomen call hell," said May Brown soberly, "because the devil 'clings' to people, tempting them to do wrong, and is generally hard to remove."

Just then, they heard a thunderous cry of rage that echoed through the whole sky. There was the sound of hooves racing toward the mansion.

"The devil is coming," said the wisewoman. She took the little brother by the hand. They hurried up to the mansion, meeting the devil in his black chariot as he came driving away from the house, the daughter cowering beside him. He looked nothing like a man now. He was glowing red with wicked black eyes, horns on his head, and cloven feet.

The devil pulled the horses to a stop when he saw them. His eyes met those of the local wisewoman. The little brother could tell at once that they knew each other. When she saw them, the daughter begged them to save her.

"Is anyone here? Anyone here?" the devil said softly, his eyes glittering. "Name of May Brown from General Cling Town."

"I am here," said the wisewoman. "My name is May Brown, but I am not from General Cling Town."

"What is whiter than any sheep's down in General Cling Town?" asked the devil.

"Snow," said the wise woman. "Snow is whiter than any sheep's down in General Cling Town."

The devil glared at her.

"What is greener than any wheat grown in General Cling Town?" he asked.

"Grass," said the wisewoman. "Grass is greener than any wheat grown in General Cling Town."

"What is bluer than anything down in General Cling Town?"

"The sky is bluer than anything down in General Cling Town," said the wisewoman.

The devil was furious. He was only allowed four riddles, and May Brown had answered the first three correctly.

"What is louder than any horns down in General Cling Town?" asked the Devil.

"Thunder is louder than any horns down in General Cling Town," said the wisewoman. The little brother knew the wisewoman had answered correctly, and so did the devil. He hopped up and down in his chariot, beside himself with rage. The devil had lost his bride.

"I will have your soul for this, May Brown," shouted the devil.

May Brown removed her shoe, tore off the sole, and threw it to the devil.

The devil caught the sole in his hands. He gripped it so hard it started to burn. The devil stared at it in disbelief. The devil thought he could claim May Brown's soul, but she had tricked him by giving him the sole of her shoe!

The devil howled, a chilling sound that haunted the little brother's dreams for the rest of his life. Then the devil threw the daughter out of his carriage. She landed at her brother's feet. The devil tossed an egg into the air. It transformed into a large bird.

"Hop and skip, Betty. Take me home," said the devil.

And with that, the devil disappeared.

25

Goggle-Eyed Jim

GREAT DISMAL SWAMP, VIRGINIA

He was a notorious scoundrel and a horse thief. And he was the bane of my existence. Goggle-Eyed Jim they called him. The things they called me when I failed to catch him . . . Well, that's beside the point.

Being the only lawman in a backcountry area close to the Great Dismal Swamp ain't easy. Too many of my suspects lost themselves in the trees and undergrowth of the swamp, leaving me behind in mud up to my armpits and with—more often than not—a lump on my head where I hit it on a low-hanging branch. It was infuriating.

But Goggle-Eyed Jim was the worst. Week after week, angry citizens would storm into my office demanding justice. Their reports were always the same. They'd been awakened by the clanging of a cowbell and a huge hullabaloo out in the barn. By the time they'd grabbed a rifle and run outside, a dark-cloaked figure with huge goggles that reflected oddly in the moonlight would flash by on the back of the citizen's best horse, laughing as he went. Goggle-Eyed Jim had a hee-haw of a laugh, like a braying donkey. But he was no laughing matter.

GOGGLE-EYED JIM

When the mayor brought home a real beaut of a stallion that October, I set up a trap for Goggle-Eyed Jim. I arranged with the mayor to sleep in his barn in the hayloft overlooking the horse stalls every night for a week. We were both sure that Goggle-Eyed Jim would come for the horse as soon as he heard about it. And the mayor made sure to parade his new purchase up and down the streets of our little town, boasting all the while of his prowess as a race horse, his beauty, his price.

Sure enough, three days later I was awakened from a strangely deep sleep by the clanging of a cowbell. I cursed and rolled over in my prickly bed of hay, throwing off my old horse blanket and reaching for my rifle. The blanket sent up a huge cloud of dust, and I sneezed as I snatched up the gun and scrambled on hands and knees to the edge of the loft. How had Goggle-Eyed Jim gotten into the barn without my hearing him? I am the lightest of sleepers, but not even the soft whicker of a horse had disturbed my slumber, though I'd been awakened by much smaller sounds on previous evenings.

As I reached the edge of the loft, I saw a horse's tail swishing through the open barn door. By now the other horses were neighing and whinnying to beat the band. Many of them reared when I made a foolish leap directly down to the floor from my perch, still clutching my rifle. I could have busted a leg but somehow made it with only a painful twist to my ankle. I rushed outside, stopping right beside the barn door to take aim at the fleeing rider with his flapping black cloak and reflecting goggle eyes. The mayor came rushing out of the house as I took my first shot, and he got off a second shot as I reloaded and aimed again.

I was sure I'd hit the scalawag with my first shot, and I know I nailed him with the second. But he kept on riding down the lane and out of sight, and the air was filled with the hee-haw of his laughter as he got away again!

The mayor was not pleased. Folks started talking about running me out of town—or hauling out the tar and feathers. I was about ready to resign when I got a real lead at last on the elusive horse thief. A fella who lived deep in the Great Dismal saw Goggle-Eyed Jim hanging out at a rickety old cabin near Lake Drummond that was once used as a hideout by pirates. As soon as he described the place, I knew exactly where he meant. I loaded up my guns and headed into the swamp in the golden afternoon light. It took a couple of hours to locate the old cabin and another couple minutes to find myself a hiding place.

Darkness fell quickly, and no Goggle-Eyed Jim. I made myself comfortable. I didn't care how long I had to wait. I'd wait until kingdom come if I had to. That darned horse thief was going to jail, and I was the one who was going to put him there.

Well, I thought I'd kept my eyes and ears open, but I must have dozed off, 'cause suddenly there was a light shining in the upstairs window and I could hear voices coming from the cabin. One of them was a woman's voice, and she was giggling and cooing like a dove. Seems like I'd caught Goggle-Eyed Jim in a tryst. Too bad for him.

I hauled out an old ladder I'd spotted in the lean-to on the side of the cabin and put it against the wall. Cradling my pistol, I climbed up the ladder and peered into the window. Yep. There he was: Goggle-Eyed Jim. He was swathed in his long black cloak and still wearing his green goggles. They seemed to glow in the lantern light—made my skin crawl. I'd be glad to see the creepy fellow behind bars.

At that moment, a lady wearing not much to speak of flounced into the room with a bottle of brandy and a couple of tin cups. She cozied up to Goggle-Eyed Jim, cooing something flirtatious into his ear.

"Right-o. Your time is up, old chap," I muttered, pulling out my pistol. The bounty on Goggle-Eyed Jim said "dead or alive," and I didn't much care which it was at that moment. He'd made my life too miserable for too long for me to feel any compassion for him.

As if he sensed my thoughts, Goggle-Eyed Jim turned his face toward the window where I crouched atop the ladder. His eyes, behind the goggles, seemed to glow with a greenish-blue light. His face was so gray and withered, he looked like a corpse. He grinned suddenly, showing a mouth with more gap than yellow teeth. I aimed and fired. I hit him too. The woman shrieked and fled, and Goggle-Eyed Jim clamped a hand over his chest and staggered dramatically toward the far window. By the time I clambered inside the cabin, he was poised on the window ledge. He gave me a jaunty wave and then tumbled out the window, still dramatically clutching his chest.

I tore down the stairs, rushing past the floozy and out into the tall grass of the yard. A figure in a dark cloak lay in the grass, his green goggles glowing in the moonlight.

"I gotcha!" I shouted, racing toward him. And then I stopped abruptly with a gasp of fear. The prone figure before me began floating upward from his grassy bed, his arms still outstretched. Goggle-Eyed Jim was . . . well, he was glowing from within! And, I realized with an ice-cold shudder, I could see the weedy lawn right through his body. He was a ghost!

By this time, Goggle-Eyed Jim was floating about six feet in the air, his body still sprawled flat on nothing. Suddenly he sat bolt upright and snorted: "Hee-Haw! Hee-Haw!"

I staggered backward with a gasp of disbelief as the ghastly figure started to spin around and around, faster and faster, still snorting with laughter. A dark hole appeared behind the glowing figure with its piercing green goggles, which were the only part of the spirit I could make out in the furious, body-blurring twirl. Suddenly the spinning figure fell backward into the dark hole, which shut with a loud snap. The empty yard was filled with the smell of sulfur.

I let out a shriek of pure, gut-wrenching terror and went crashing away into the woods. Behind me, the floozy let out an equally loud shriek and went crashing off in the other direction. I'd run only about a hundred steps before I broke through a tangle of bushes into a hidden meadow and was nearly trampled by the mayor's stallion, which had been happily grazing in the moonlight until I came crashing along.

The stallion wasn't the only horse in the meadow. There were at least six more horses, all of them reported stolen by Goggle-Eyed Jim. I stared at the horses in wonder. Just how long had Goggle-Eyed Jim been a ghost?

Casting my mind back over the reported thefts and matching them up to the horses before me, I reckoned that the horse thief had been dead at least six months. Not that this small detail had fazed Goggle-Eyed Jim. He'd just kept right on stealing horses, though he had no need to sell them now. No wonder bullets didn't affect him! I knew both my shots had landed that night at the mayor's house.

Standing there in that moonlit meadow, my skin still crawling from my encounter with the ghost, I wondered how I was going to explain the situation to the mayor. Then I shrugged, mounted the stallion bareback, and rode home. I'd return for the other horses in the morning.

The mayor was mighty glad to get his horse back, though he wasn't terribly convinced by my story about the ghostly Goggle-Eyed Jim. Still, once he'd seen all them horses grazing in the hidden meadow, he decided at least part of my story must be true. Anyhow, he okayed my plan to have a priest out to the old cabin to do an exorcism. And that did the trick. Goggle-Eyed Jim's days of horse thieving were over. And I got to keep my job. So one of us had a happy ending. I'm glad it was me!

26

The Witch Woman and the Spinning Wheel

NEW ORLEANS, LOUISIANA

Moses was living just outside of New Orleans, way back before the Civil War. Moses made a pretty good living assisting the local blacksmith, and he was right pleased with his life, but he missed the company of a good woman. Mostly, he wanted a wife because he was such a bad cook. But all the ladies who caught his fancy were already promised to someone else, and the ones who weren't seemed like they just wanted his money. So Moses stayed single.

One evening, Moses was out late, hunting in the swamp. He was mighty tired and hungry and far from home when he came to a clearing with a small cabin. The clearing was filled with the most delicious fragrances Moses had ever smelled: cornpone and rabbit meat and some sort of cake. Moses's mouth started watering.

"I don't care what I gotta pay," Moses told his horse. "I'm gonna get me some of that food."

THE WITCH WOMAN AND THE SPINNING WHEEL

A pretty little lady came hurrying out of the cabin when she saw his horse. She was spry as a bird and had big, sparkling black eyes.

"You look tired and hungry. Come in and have some supper," she called to Moses.

Moses was happy to do so. He tied up his horse and went into the cabin, eyeing the skillet on the coals. The lady was real pretty, and the food was awful good. Moses ate until he was stuffed so full he couldn't move, and he enjoyed the whole evening with the pretty lady.

Moses was awful distracted the next day at the smithy. He kept thinking about that good food and the pretty lady who prepared it. So, he went back to see her that evening. She fed him and flattered him, and Moses just ate and ate. He was going to get mighty fat if he kept eating that good. The idea appealed to Moses. He kept visiting the pretty lady, and one day they got married, and Moses moved into the cabin at the edge of the swamp.

Moses started bringing home all his money to the pretty lady, keeping her in comfort and style. And she fed him good. Moses was happy with his life, but his new wife was awful strict with him. She made him come home right after work and wouldn't let him have a drink or two with his friends. And she was always spending all his money, so there was none left for him. But she was such a good cook that Moses put up with her ways.

But one thing puzzled Moses about his new wife. Whenever he woke in the middle of the night, his wife would be missing from the cabin. Moses didn't know where she went at night, and it didn't seem fair to him that she made him stay home after work while she went gallivanting around.

So, Moses decided to spy on his wife. That night he lay down on the bed in the corner and pretended to sleep. Once his wife heard him snoring, she got up and put a gridiron next to the hearth. Then she got out her spinning wheel and put it next to the gridiron. As soon as the gridiron was red hot, she sat on the gridiron and started spinning the wheel with her hand. Moses was horrified. Only a witch could sit on a red-hot gridiron. And Moses knew of only one reason for a witch to heat herself up: She was going to transform herself!

His wife began to chant, "Turn and spin, come off skin. Turn and spin, come off skin."

She plucked a thread of skin from the top of her head and spun it onto the spinning wheel. As Moses watched in amazement, his wife's skin shucked off as easily as husk from an ear of corn. Underneath her skin was the body of a great big yellow cat. When she was finished, the cat took the skin and tossed it under the bed where Moses lay.

"Stay there, skin, till I get back. I'm gonna have some fun," said the big yellow cat. Then she jumped out the window and loped into the night.

When she was gone, Moses sat up in bed. He was horrified. He had married a witch! She must have put a spell on him the first time he came to her cabin. Moses wanted to run to the preacher right away and make sure he was still going to heaven. But first, he had to do something about that witch.

Moses grabbed the skin out from under the bed. He poured pepper and salt onto the skin until it was covered. Then he tossed it back under the bed, grabbed his clothes and his money, and ran out the back door.

Moses hid in the woods and waited a long time for the witch to come home. When the big yellow cat came into the clearing and jumped through the window, Moses snuck up to the cabin and put his eye to a crack in the wall. He wanted to make sure that the witch was taken care of before he went to see the preacher.

Well, that witch was all cackling and happy after her night out. She laughed as she ran over to the empty bed and grabbed up the skin and shook herself into it. But when she felt the salt and pepper in the skin, she started to scream and scream. She twisted and turned, trying to get the skin off. Smoke started coming off her body, and she writhed in agony until she dropped down dead.

At once, Moses felt the spell lift from his mind. He was horrified at how close he'd come to going to hell with that witch woman. Moses ran and ran all the way into town and roused the preacher out of his bed. Once the preacher heard his story, he told Moses what a narrow escape he had had, and they prayed that the good Lord would forgive Moses and not send him to hell.

Moses went back to living at the smithy, where he had slept in the loft until his marriage. He didn't ever look at a woman again, even though he had to eat his own bad cooking the rest of his days.

27

Jack-o'-Lantern

WHEELER NATIONAL WILDLIFE REFUGE, ALABAMA

When I was just a young boy living down in Alabama with my grandpappy, he told me about the googly-eyed jack-o'-lantern that bounds across the swamps. Folks walking in the dark swamp at night had best be careful or the jack-o'-lantern will lure them with his light. Folks say that once you've seen the jack-o'-lantern, you get this irresistible impulse to follow him wherever he goes. You follow the light until you fall into bogs or pools of water and drown.

"Tommy," my grandpappy used to say, "the only way to resist the jack-o'-lantern when you see him is to turn your coat and your pockets inside out. That will confuse him and he'll leave you alone. If you're not wearing a coat, then you should carry a new knife that's never cut wood. Like many evil creatures, the jack-o'-lantern doesn't like newly forged steel, and he'll keep away."

"Grandpappy, where'd the jack-o'-lantern come from?" I asked him once.

"Well now," said my grandpappy, "I hear tell that Jack was once a man who wanted power and riches. One night he went to the crossroads at midnight, and he made a deal with the devil.

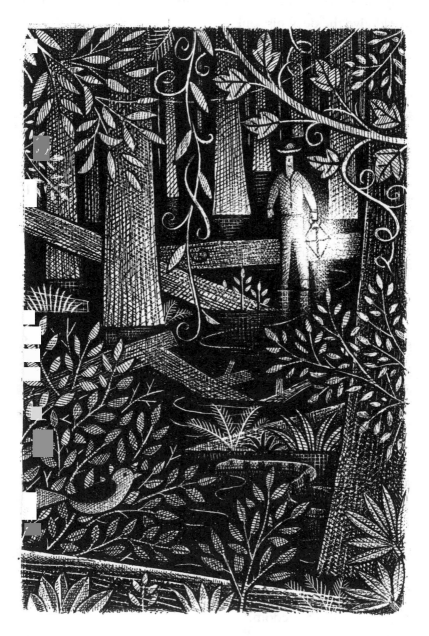

JACK-O'-LANTERN

If the devil made him rich and famous, then in seven years Jack would give the devil his soul.

"The devil was mighty pleased with this agreement. He gave Jack just what he wanted. Jack grew rich and famous, and he married a beautiful girl and was as happy as could be for seven years.

"Then one night the devil came to claim Jack's soul. Now Jack had had seven years to figure out how to weasel out of his bargain with the devil, and he was prepared. He had tacked the sole of an old shoe over his front door.

On the night the devil showed up, Jack acted as if he was all set to keep his part of the bargain, that is, to turn over his soul and accompany the devil to hell. But suddenly Jack smacked his forehead with his hand and said, 'Wait! I thought if I hid my soul you wouldn't be able to find me. But now that you have, I might as well bring it along.'

"The devil was annoyed with Jack for hiding his soul. 'Where is it?' he asked, not realizing this was a trick.

'Over the door,' said Jack, pointing up at the sole of the old shoe.

"When the devil stood up on a chair and reached for the sole, Jack jumped up quick with a hammer and some nails and nailed the devil's hand to the doorpost.

" 'Aiiii!' yelled the devil as Jack slipped the chair out from under his feet. 'Get me down from here!'

" 'Sorry, Devil, but you're stuck up there,' said Jack.

" 'What do you want from me?' asked the devil.

" 'I want my freedom.'

" 'We made a bargain,' the devil said, swinging to and fro from his stuck hand.

" 'And I nailed you to my doorpost. So what will it be?' asked Jack.

" 'All right then,' said the devil. 'You've got your freedom.'

"My, but the devil was grumpy at having been tricked by Jack. Jack got the Devil down from the doorpost, and the devil stomped away. And Jack lived to a ripe old age with his beautiful wife and his fine sons and his nice house.

"But when Jack died and went up to heaven, those angels in charge of them pearly gates said, 'You can't come in here, Jack. You struck a bargain with the devil. You'd best be getting on to hell.'

"No matter how Jack argued with the angels, they wouldn't let him into heaven. So finally Jack went down to hell to see the devil. Jack was mighty scared to visit hell, seeing as he tricked the devil so bad during his lifetime.

"Well, Jack knocked on the other gates—the bad ones—and the devil looked out at him.

" 'Who's there?' asked the devil, even though the devil sure enough knew it was Jack.

" 'It's your old friend Jack,' said Jack.

" 'I don't have a friend Jack,' said the devil. 'My friend Jack tricked me and we're not friends anymore.'

" 'Come on, devil, let me in,' said Jack. 'I've got no place else to go. They won't let me into heaven.'

" 'You don't belong in heaven,' said the devil. 'And you don't belong here either.'

" 'Go away and don't come back here,' said the devil. 'You're too smart for hell.'

" 'Where will I go? And how will I see in the darkness?' Jack asked desperately.

"The devil threw a chunk of brimstone at Jack. 'Use this to see. I don't care where you go, as long as it isn't here.'

"Well now, Jack didn't have any place else to go. He wasn't allowed in heaven and he wasn't welcome in hell. He bitterly regretted the trick he had played on the devil, but it was too late. So Jack picked up the chunk of brimstone and came back to earth.

He put the brimstone into an old lantern he found to keep it from blowing out in the wind and used it to light his way through the dark marshes and swamps where he preferred to walk. From that day to this, a bitter and angry jack-o'-lantern wanders the earth, luring people into the swamps and mud holes. Jack's taking out his vengeance on us poor sinners because no one will let him into heaven or hell."

My grandpappy and I sat in silence for a moment after he finished the story. Then my grandpappy looked at me and said, "And that, Johnny, is why you should always carry a new knife when you're walking through the swamp. The jack-o'-lantern doesn't like newly forged steel, so he stays away."

And that's why I always do.

28

Plat-Eye

HARRISON COUNTY, MISSISSIPPI

Now don't you be scoffing at the plat-eye. I'm telling you that plat-eyes are no laughing matter. They're evil spirits that haunt the woods and swamps of Mississippi. They can take the form of any animal, and they attack people walking alone in solitary places. If you meet a creature that has fiery eyes, you'd better run the other way, because it's not an animal, it's a plat-eye.

How do I come to know about plat-eyes, you ask? Well, child, I met one once when I was still young and pretty, that's how. Oh, so now you want to hear the story, do you? Well, grab a stool and try some of these molasses cookies I made for you, and I'll tell you about it.

I was sweethearting with your grandpa back then. He lived close to the shore in those days, and that evening I just so happened to pass his house on my way to gather clams at low tide. Well, he abandoned his chores when he saw me go by. That foolish boy just haunted my steps, hampering me at every turn and whispering sweet things in my ear.

It was getting dark, and your great-grandpa saw your grandpa walking me home and yelled for him to come back and help with the cows. Your grandpa was reluctant to leave me, but

PLAT-EYE

I told him that I'd been walking down the lane all my life so he didn't need to play muscle man for me. He was a bit huffed by my attitude, and he didn't try to kiss me goodnight before he went down to the barn to help his pa. I didn't mind. Your grandpa was pretty cocky in those days, and I tried to keep him on his toes. I didn't want him to be too sure of me just yet.

I kept walking home alone. It was a right pretty night and I was enjoying the walk, not scared or anything. After all, it was true what I told your grandpa. I'd walked down the lane my whole life and nothing had ever happened to me.

In those days, the road home led through a thick wood, and there was a footbridge—just an old log, really—across the stream toward the center of the trees. I looked up as I approached it, and there was a black cat, its eyes like blazing fire and all its hair standing up on its back. It was arched up like it was spitting-mad, and its tail was a-switching and a-twitching. That cat moved right in front of me, standing in the center of the cypress log. As soon as I saw its blazing eyes, I knew that the cat was what my granny called a "plat-eye": an evil spirit that haunted the Mississippi woods. It was just as big as a baby ox, and I was feeling mighty nervous looking at him. But I said aloud, "I'm not afraid of anything, no sir. Not any ghost. Not any plat-eye. Nothing!"

That plat-eye didn't say a word to me; it just moved forward, its tail lashing back and forth. I gripped the short-handled clam rake in my hand and started singing a hymn: "God will take care of me, Walking through many dangers."

Well, I seemed to hear a voice in my head reminding me that the Lord takes care of those who help themselves. So I raised the rake and brought it crashing down on the head of that cat. If it had been a real cat, I would have pinned it to that log. But it was a plat-eye, no mistake, and it didn't even feel the blow. I was young then, remember, and my pa had taught me how to hit out at dangerous critters. But that plat-eye was just as frisky after I hit it as before.

I was cussing at it, and hitting it with the rake, and saying, "You devil! Clear my path!" But the cursed thing just pawed the air and tried to jump on me. I ducked and it hit a vine next to me. And in my mind I heard another voice saying: "Child of God, travel the wood path!" That seemed like good advice, so I turned back and made haste back up the lane.

Just when I was thanking God for getting me clear of that plat-eye, there it was again. Now it was big as a middle-size ox, and its eyes were blazing bright enough to light up the woods on either side of the path. I smashed at it with my rake, dumped my bucket of clams over its head, and took off running as quick as I could. I looked behind me once to see if it was still coming, and I saw that the plat-eye was now as big as my cousin Andrew's full-grown ox, and its eyes were bright as the noonday sun. So I ran as fast as I could, praying to the good Lord to spare me. As I broke out of the deep wood, that plat-eye veered off the lane and vanished up into the old box pine at the edge of the forest.

I kept running till I couldn't run anymore, and then I walked along toward your grandpa's house just gasping and crying. I met him halfway there. He was coming after me to make sure I had gotten home safe. I just fell into his arms and cried.

After hearing my story, your grandpa took me back to his farm and got us some gunpowder and sulfur. The plat-eyes can't stand the smells of gunpowder and sulfur when they're mixed. At least, that's what Uncle Murphy—the witch doctor in those parts—had told your grandpa. Then your grandpa got a big stick and prayed to the good Lord to protect us, and he walked me home down the lane.

When we got under the old box pine, he mixed up the gunpowder and sulfur so it stank up the air, and he waved his big stick and threatened to beat the plat-eye to death if it ever came near his girl again. But the plat-eye didn't appear. We found my empty bucket and the clam rake right near the footbridge, and we walked safe and sound right up to my door. And before we said goodnight, your grandpa made me promise never to walk alone in the woods without taking some gunpowder and sulfur along and carrying a big stick.

And I never did.

Roses

In the end, what enraged him more than the love affair itself was the way they assumed he had the intelligence of a wooden post. Did they think he wouldn't notice the way his wife lit up whenever his first officer entered the room or the way the first officer followed her with his eyes? Obviously, they thought he was too stupid to realize how they both just happened to disappear at the same time and that when they reappeared, she was glowing and his uniform smelled of rose perfume. It was infuriating!

His father had warned him against taking such a flirtatious, pretty woman to wife. She would stray, he had said, and, devil curse him, his father had been right. And his men were laughing at him behind his back. They knew what was going on. Oh, yes they did. He was a laughingstock because of his wife and his first officer, and it was going to stop tonight. He would make sure of it.

When his wife swept into his commandant's quarters in the Castillo, he was seated at his desk, apparently absorbed in paperwork. She had been pouting for days, ever since he'd sent his first officer south to the Caribbean with an important

ROSES

commission that would keep him away from the Castillo for more than two years. She flounced into a chair and glared at him in petty anger.

"Well?" she said peevishly when he refused to look up. He glanced at the door and nodded to the night guard who stood there. The man tactfully withdrew from the room, closing the heavy door behind him.

He leaned back in his chair, his nostrils twitching as the cloying scent of her rose perfume filled the room. "Well, my dear. It seems we are at an impasse," he said. "I am happy working in this New World, but you are not happy living here. Or should I say you are not happy living here with me?"

His wife looked up sharply, going a little pale at the tone of his voice. She searched his eyes, trying to see what, if anything, he knew about her and her lover.

"What nonsense have you got in your head?" she asked, trying to sound playful—and failing. "I am perfectly happy here with you!"

"You have not seemed so these last few months," said the commandant. He rose from his seat and beckoned to his wife. "However, perhaps the surprise I have for you will mend matters. Come, walk with me."

"A surprise for me?" asked his wife, half delighted and half suspicious.

She rose with a dubious smile on her red lips, and he bowed her through the door into the outer chamber, where the night guard stood to attention.

As the commandant took his wife's arm, he said loudly, "There is a ship in the harbor that leaves for Spain at first light, my dear. I am sure the captain would be happy to oblige us when we explain the situation to him."

His wife gave him a puzzled glance at this sudden change of topic, but it was not for her benefit that he broached it. He saw the guard start a little and then school his face to impassivity as they swept out into the courtyard, arm in arm. The commandant smiled grimly. The night guard would certainly pass along what he'd heard to the other men, fueling the speculation about the commandant and his unfaithful wife.

"What was all that about a ship?" his wife demanded petulantly as they crossed the courtyard.

"It's all part of the surprise," he told her soothingly as he led her to an unused storeroom and escorted her inside.

"Why are we here?" his wife demanded sharply, staring at the broken pieces of furniture and dusty wooden crates that filled the room. "This is no place to hide a gift."

"On the contrary, my dear," said the commandant happily. "It is the perfect place to hide something."

So saying, he led her to a concealed opening in the wall. His wife stared at it. "What is that?" she asked suspiciously. "Why have I never seen it before?"

"It is a hidden room I discovered some time ago," said the commandant. "It is a place to store secret things."

He lifted the torch from its socket beside the storeroom door and went to the dark opening. With a smile, he gestured for his wife to precede him into the secret room. The scent of her rose perfume filled the air as she stepped inside to see her surprise.

At dawn the next morning, the commandant stood on the pier, waving good-bye to the ship bound for Spain. When the ship disappeared over the horizon, he strolled thoughtfully back to the Castillo and explained to his men that his wife had left for Spain to tend her ailing father. The soldiers exchanged looks, but none of them said anything in front of him. However, he knew that among themselves they would spread a different tale—one that claimed the commandant had discovered his wife's affair with the first officer and had separated the lovers, sending the officer to the Caribbean and banishing her to Spain for her infidelity. The commandant didn't care what the gossips said. What mattered was that his unfaithful wife and her lover were gone, and he was a free man.

A few months later, the commandant resigned his position and left the Castillo for good. He left behind only vague rumors about his wife's scandalous love affair that had gone awry.

Fifty years swiftly passed away, and the story of the commandant's unfaithful wife had faded from the memory of the townspeople. Florida was now part of the United States, and the Castillo had become Fort Marion. New faces and new concerns filled the stone rooms and towers, and one of those faces belonged to Sergeant Tuttle. On this particular day, his main concern was moving some old cannons around the upper gun deck, not an easy task at the best of times.

"Heave," he told his men.

"Heave!" they answered, doing so.

CRASH went the cannon, right through the floor.

"Holy Moses!" shouted Tuttle, staring down into the huge hole that had opened in the floor of the gun deck. He could barely make out the cannon at the bottom amidst the dust, debris, and filtered sunlight. "What a god-awful mess! You men, get down there right now!" he added, pointing to the two men closest to the stairs.

The men hurried down the stairs and into the room below the gun deck, only to find it devoid of debris. There was no mess, no cannon, no dust. Nothing was amiss.

The men stared wide eyed at each other and then checked the adjoining rooms. Still nothing. Where was the dang-blasted cannon?

The two men ran back up to the gun deck to inform Tuttle of the disappearing cannon. The sergeant, still staring down the hole, commented that it was taking his men far too long to appear. He jumped a mile when one of them spoke at his elbow.

"Sarge, we can't find the cannon," the man reported. Tuttle jerked upright and whirled around. "What do you mean you can't find the cannon?" he roared. "It's right there!" He gestured into the hole.

"It may be right there," said the man, quaking but defiant, "but it isn't down there!" He gestured to the room below. The two men dragged Tuttle downstairs and showed him the empty room. By this time, most of the men working on the gun deck had followed them downstairs, so there was quite a crowd when the sergeant pronounced, "There must be a sealed chamber behind that wall. Men, we need pickaxes and sledgehammers."

Immediately the soldiers dispersed to locate the requested tools, and soon several men were hammering away at the coquina wall with a will, speculating between blows about the reason the newly christened cannon room had been sealed.

As the first hammer penetrated the secret room, the air was suddenly filled with an overwhelming scent of roses. A moment later, the hole was big enough to peer inside. The men ripped away at the hole until there was room to enter the hidden chamber. Grabbing a lantern, Tuttle stepped into the secret space, followed by his men. There, amid the dust and rubble, stood the fallen cannon. And behind it, chained to the wall, were two moldering skeletons. One still wore the decaying remains of a first officer's uniform. The other still smelled faintly of roses.

30

The Witch Bridle

ALBRIGHT, WEST VIRGINIA

Well now, old Ebenezer Braham learned a lesson about dealing with witches, one night last summer, and it's one he won't ever forget, no sir. Ebenezer was living at the time in a one-room log cabin outside Albright near the Cheat River. The cabin didn't have too much in the way of furnishings, just a great big old fireplace in one corner and his little bed in the other. Ebenezer was a simple man.

One night Ebenezer woke up, hearing men's voices talking right there in his cabin. He didn't know where the men had come from, but he figured it was best to pretend he was still sleeping until he learned what was going on. He listened carefully, and to his astonishment, he learned that the voices belonged to men who were members of a band of witches. They were using his house to store their bewitched bridles.

From the bits of conversation he overheard, Ebenezer realized that the men could use the bridles on man or beast, who would then be subjected to the witches' will, carrying the witches like horses wherever they wanted to go. That night, these witches wanted to go to the witch feast up on Scraggle Mountain, and they were going to ride Ebenezer's calves all the

THE WITCH BRIDLE

way up there and back. Ebenezer was real sore when he heard that. He was proud of those calves. One of them was sure to win him prizes at the local fair.

One of the witches—the seventh one—was missing from the group that night. The witches complained bitterly about his defection, and Ebenezer cracked open one of his eyes to get a glimpse at them while they were deep in conversation. He watched as they took the witch bridles and a magic ointment out from under the hearthstone. He saw them rub the ointment on their foreheads and throats, cross themselves three times, and fly up the chimney.

Ebenezer jumped out of bed and watched from the window as the witches placed the bridles on six of his seven calves and rode them away toward Scraggle Mountain. Well, Ebenezer decided to do something foolish. He had never been to a witches' feast, and here was one witch bridle and the magic ointment right under his hearthstone. He would never have a better opportunity than this. So Ebenezer moved the heavy hearthstone and grabbed the last witch bridle. Then he took the ointment, rubbed it on his forehead and throat, crossed himself three times, and flew right up the chimney with a startled yell of delight.

Ebenezer landed in the calf lot and bridled up the last calf, a small red one. He jumped up on its back and urged the small animal to its top speed. He wanted to follow those witch men to the feast, and they had a head start on him. The little red calf was as fast as the wind. Before you could say Jack Robinson, Ebenezer could see the witch men ahead of him at the ford. The men urged the calves to jump the stream. The calves all made the leap with ease, except the small white calf, which landed in the water on the far side of the stream. That calf had to wade out and climb the steep bank on the other side, but soon it was running merrily behind the others, its rider just a little bit wet.

Ebenezer knew his calf was even smaller than the white one, but it had run so fast that he was sure it could make the jump. So Ebenezer urged his calf forward. The brave little red calf jumped as high as it could, but it landed on a log that had been submerged smack in the center of the stream. The log split in two, and Ebenezer barely managed to grab hold of it with one hand and the witch bridle with the other. The bit of the witch bridle slid out of the mouth of the calf, and the little animal disappeared beneath the water.

Ebenezer was angry and wet. He dragged himself onto the log belly first. But before he could stand, SMACK! something jumped on his back and WHAM! something pushed the witch bridle into his mouth. Ebenezer barely got a glimpse of a large blue cat before it mounted him, shouting, "Haha! I will get a ride to the witches' feast after all. Too bad about your calf, Ebenezer. If you hadn't pushed him to jump, I would have ridden him instead of you. Haha!"

The big blue cat twitched the reins and slapped Ebenezer in the face with one big blue paw. Ebenezer was terribly mad, but he was under the spell of that witch bridle, so all he could do was crawl off toward Scraggle Mountain on his hands and knees like a horse. That big blue cat was a mean one. It jumped up and down on Ebenezer's back, urging him to go faster. It whipped him with the reins and beat him with its claws and jerked the bit back and forth in Ebenezer's mouth until his teeth ached. Up and up they climbed over terribly sharp rocks, hard roots, and bumpy ground.

"Hahaha!" the cat laughed. "Hahaha!"

At last, they drew near the witches' meeting place on Scraggle Mountain, and the big blue cat tied Ebenezer like a horse, so it could ride him back down the mountain when the feasting was over. While the big blue cat went off to revel with the other witches, Ebenezer tried and tried to shake the witch bridle's control over his mind. He was still trying when the big blue cat returned to the place Ebenezer was tied. The cat was yawning sleepily.

"I'm gonna take a nap before I ride you home, haha!" said the blue cat to Ebenezer. It curled up under the tree next to Ebenezer and fell asleep immediately. Somehow, the sight of the terrible blue cat did the trick. Suddenly Ebenezer's mind was clear, and he pulled off the witch bridle. Gazing angrily at the blue cat, Ebenezer decided it was his turn for a ride. He snuck up on the cat and thrust the bridle over its head and put the bit in its mouth. Ruthlessly, he shook the cat awake. The big blue cat snarled and hit out at Ebenezer with its claws, but Ebenezer just laughed.

"Hohoho! I was your horse up the mountain, now you can be my horse down the mountain. And you've got the easier piece, 'cause it's all downhill from here. So I guess you'll have to take me all the way home to make it even."

The cat yowled and pleaded with Ebenezer, but in the end it had to carry him down the mountain. Ebenezer was a big, heavy man, and the cat's paws were scratched and bleeding by the time they reached the bottom of the mountain. The blue cat groaned and complained at the weight of its burden.

They were nearly back to Ebenezer's house when the blue cat turned aside and tried to carry Ebenezer toward an old dilapidated hut. Ebenezer was feeling happier now, content that he had avenged himself sufficiently on the terrible blue cat. He decided to let it go and walk the rest of the way home. He dismounted, but kept the witch bridle firmly in place as the blue cat hobbled toward the door. As soon as the blue cat reached the hut, it was transformed into an evil old witch woman.

"Hahaha!" she cackled at Ebenezer. "Now you see who I really am! I am going to bewitch you until you die, Ebenezer."

"Hohoho!" said Ebenezer. "I still have the witch bridle on you and I am still your rider. I'm going to chain you to the wall and go home to make a silver bullet. Then I'll come back and shoot you."

The witch woman wailed and pleaded for Ebenezer to spare her life, but Ebenezer chained her up and went home with the witch bridle to make a silver bullet.

Well, just after sunrise, a man came to the dilapidated hut to plead with the witch to spare the life of his son, whom the witch had cursed the previous evening. When the man saw that the witch was chained, he thought he should go away. Someone was obviously going to take care of that evil witch, and then his son would be free of the curse.

But the witch, seeing a chance at freedom, beguiled the man by claiming that her death would not remove the curse from his son. If the man set her free, she said, she would remove the curse and promise never to harm the man or his family again. As proof of her goodwill, she offered the man a gold ring she had in her pocket. So the man found a sharp stone and broke the chain holding her to the wall. He left the hut with an antidote for his son and the gold ring in his pocket.

"Hahaha! I will deal with you later," the witch called softly after his departing figure. "Right now, I have another spell to make."

The witch pulled out the shining tin pan she used for spells from her crooked wooden cupboard and sat down in the blazing sunshine. She gazed unblinking into the brightness of the tin; her evil eyes were used to the glare after many years of spell-making. She began to chant the spell, calling on the devil to help her bewitch Ebenezer Braham.

"He shall be in pain," she said. "Terrible pain." With her finger, the witch drew figures on the blazing tin pan and tapped the pan several times.

At his home, Ebenezer was nearly finished making the silver bullet. As a precaution, he had also drawn the likeness of the witch on a piece of paper. He could feel the witch's spell trying to take him, so he hurriedly put the silver bullet into his gun. Then he ran outside, fixed the picture of the witch to a tree, took aim, and fired. The silver bullet struck the center of the picture and slammed deeply into the tree.

In the doorway of the hut, the witch was finishing her spell. "Pain shall plague Ebenezer Braham henceforth until he dies, so help me de- . . . "

It was at that critical moment that the bullet pierced the center of the picture. The witch gave a terrible cry, dropped the glowing tin pan, and clapped her hand to her heart.

"I am shot! I am killed!" she screamed, and fell over dead.

Ebenezer felt the spell lift from his mind. He bent in half, breathing deeply until he calmed down again. Then he went to the hearthstone, withdrew the witch bridles that the witches had returned in the night, and burned them in a hot, hot fire until they were completely gone. He placed a copy of the Good Book under the hearthstone, and the witches never came to his house again.

But Ebenezer kept the magic ointment, and once in a while he will still fly up the chimney and soar like a bird over the countryside until dawn.

31

Tailypo

Way back in the woods of Tennessee lived an old man and his three dogs—Uno, Ino, and Cumptico-Calico. They lived in a small cabin with only one room. This room was their parlor and their bedroom and their kitchen and their sitting room. It had one giant fireplace where the old man cooked supper for himself and his dogs every night.

One night, while the dogs were snoozing by the fire and the old man was washing up after his supper, a very curious creature crept through a crack between the logs of the cabin. The old man stopped washing his plate and stared at the creature. It had a rather round body and the longest tail you ever did see.

As soon as the old man saw that varmint invading his cozy cabin, he grabbed his hatchet. Thwack! He cut off its tail. The creature gave a startled squeak and raced back through the crack in the logs. Beside the fire, the dogs grumbled a bit and rolled over, ignoring the whole thing.

The old man picked up the very long tail. There was some good meat on that tail, so he roasted it over the fire. Cumptico-Calico woke up when she smelled the tail cooking and begged for a bite, but after the old man had his first taste,

TAILYPO

he couldn't bear to part with a single mouthful. Cumptico-Calico grumbled and lay back down to sleep.

The old man was tired, so he finished washing up and went to bed. He hadn't been sleeping too long when a thumping noise awoke him. It sounded like an animal was climbing up the side of his cabin. He heard a scratch, scratch, scratching noise, like the claws of a cat. And then a voice rang out: "Tailypo, Tailypo; all I want's my Tailypo."

The old man sat bolt upright in bed. He called to the dogs, "Hut! Hut! Hut!" like he did when they were out hunting. Uno and Ino jumped up immediately and began barking like mad. Cumptico-Calico got up slowly and stretched. She was still mad at the old man for not giving her a bite of the tail. The old man sent the dogs outside. He heard them trying to climb the cabin walls after the creature. It gave a squeal and he heard a thump as it jumped to the ground and raced away, the dogs chasing it around the back of the cabin and deep into the woods.

Much later, he heard the dogs return and lay down under the lean-to attached to the cabin. The old man relaxed then and went back to sleep. Along about midnight, the old man woke with his heart pounding madly. He could hear something scratch, scratch, scratching right above his cabin door. "Tailypo, Tailypo; all I want's my Tailypo." The voice was chanting rhythmically against the steady scratch, scratch, scratch at the top of the door.

The old man jumped up, yelling, "Hut! Hut! Hut!" to his dogs. They started barking wildly, and he heard them race around the corner of the house from the lean-to. He saw them catch up with a shadowy something at the gate in front of the cabin. The dogs almost tore the fence down trying to get at it. Finally Cumptico-Calico leapt onto a stump and over the fence, Uno and Ino on her heels, and he heard them chasing the creature way down into the big swamp.

The old man sat up for a while, listening for the dogs to return. About three in the morning, he finally fell asleep again. Toward daybreak, but while it was still dark, the old man was wakened again by the sound of a voice coming from the direction of the swamp. "You know, I know; all I want's my Tailypo." The old man broke out in a cold sweat and yelled, "Hut! Hut! Hut!" for his dogs. But the dogs didn't answer, and the old man feared that the creature had lured them down into the big swamp to kill them. He got out of bed and barricaded the door. Then he hid under the covers and tried to sleep. When it was light, he was going to take his hatchet and his gun and go find his dogs.

Just before morning, the old man was wakened from a fitful doze by a thumping sound right in the cabin. Something was climbing the covers at the foot of his bed. He peered over the covers and saw two pointed ears at the end of the bed. He could hear a scratch, scratch, scratching sound as the creature climbed up the bed, and in a moment he was looking into two big, round, fiery eyes. The old man wanted to shout for the dogs, but he couldn't make his voice work. He just shivered as the creature crept up the bed toward him. It was large and heavy. He could feel its sharp claws pricking him as it walked up his body. When it reached his face, it bent toward him and said in a low voice, "Tailypo, Tailypo; all I want's my Tailypo."

All at once, the old man found his voice and he yelled, "I ain't got your Tailypo!" And the creature said, "Yes you do!" And it grabbed the old man in its claws and tore him to pieces.

The next day, a trapper came across the old man's dogs wandering aimlessly on the other side of the swamp. When the trapper brought the dogs back to the log cabin, he found the old man dead. All that remained were a few scraps of clothing and some grisly bones. As the trapper buried the old man, he heard a faint chuckling sound coming from the swamp, and a voice said, "Now I got my Tailypo." When they heard the voice, the dogs turned tail and ran for their lives.

There's nothing left of that old cabin now except the stone chimney. Folks who live nearby don't like to go there at night, because when the moon is shining brightly and the wind blows across the swamp, sometimes you can still hear a voice saying, "Tailypo."

32

The Devil's Mansion

NEW ORLEANS, LOUISIANA

I thought it very unfair that everyone stopped talking about the mansion on St. Charles Avenue whenever I came into the room. I was twelve years old the year Mama became friends with Mrs. Jacques, and I considered myself quite grown-up. Mama wouldn't let me put up my hair yet, but I did have one or two party dresses that were fancy enough for a debutante. In just a few short years I would be gracing the ballrooms of New Orleans and breaking young men's hearts. So I felt quite peeved that no one would tell me what was wrong with that mansion.

I had driven past the mansion several times while making calls with Mama, and I thought it was a beautiful house, although there was a ghastly head fixed to the gable of the roof. I could never get a clear glimpse of it because Mama made the coachman hurry past the house whenever we drove down St. Charles Avenue. I kept asking Mama and Papa to tell me about the house, but they always said they would tell me when I was older. They must have instructed the servants not to answer my questions either, because my governess refused to speak of the mansion, and I couldn't even wheedle the story out of Sarah Jane, who used to be my nanny.

THE DEVIL'S MANSION

"Elizabeth, 'tis no use your asking me about that mansion," Sarah Jane said to me, "'cause I won't tell you anything about it. It's not a story for a young girl like you."

And that was all she would say.

But after Charles Larendon passed away, the Jacqueses purchased the stately mansion on St. Charles Avenue, and Mrs. Jacques was a good friend of my mother's. So sooner or later we would have to pay a social call at the mansion. I was afraid Mama would leave me behind when she went to call on Mrs. Jacques in her new home, but Mrs. Jacques must have reassured Mama that there was nothing there to harm her only child, because Mama took me with her.

When the coach pulled up in front of the house, I got my first clear look at the strange head on the gable. It was a gruesome piece of sculpture with an angry face, two horns just above the forehead, and eyes that seemed to look right into your soul. The head appeared to be almost real, and it made my skin crawl. I hurried after Mama. The door was opened by the butler, who showed us into a very beautiful sitting room where Mrs. Jacques was entertaining callers. I looked around as best I could while we were being escorted to the sitting room. The mansion was as lovely inside as I thought it would be, but it seemed completely unexceptional. Except for the gruesome head on the gable, there was nothing that seemed out of the ordinary here.

Mrs. Jacques greeted us with delight and introduced us to the other callers. We spent quite some time there and did not leave until after tea. When we left the mansion, I was no closer to knowing what was wrong than when we arrived.

I don't think I would have ever learned the secret of the mansion if Mrs. Jacques hadn't invited the family over for dinner one evening. I was rather surprised when the dinner was served in a small family dining room that had once been a large sitting room. It seemed rather inconvenient to crowd so many people into such a small room, but Mrs. Jacques explained that her formal dining room was being renovated.

After dinner, the ladies excused themselves while the men drank port around the table. We went into Mrs. Jacques's sitting room and drank tea. While Mama and Mrs. Jacques were discussing the latest scandal, I slipped away, determined to have a good look around the mansion. I headed immediately toward the dining room. Mrs. Jacques's story about the renovation just hadn't rung true. She seemed very nervous when she mentioned the dining room. I took a candelabra from a side table and crept into the room, closing the door carefully behind me. The large room was completely empty. I stood staring about in disappointment. Mrs. Jacques had been telling the truth about the renovation, I decided, turning back toward the door.

And then the room lit up. I turned, my hand on the doorknob. Two brilliantly lit crystal chandeliers had appeared out of nowhere. Below them was a large dining-room table filled with mouthwatering things to eat. I stared in wonder as a beautiful young woman wearing an expensive if rather old-fashioned dress came in with a handsome young man. They sat down to eat, waited upon by silent servants while they held a silent conversation with one another.

The candelabra in my hands started to shake as I realized that I was seeing ghosts. I wanted to run away, but I was frozen to the spot. At the table, the young man was talking earnestly to the young woman. As I watched, her face turned pale with fear and anger. She started to shout at the young man, although there was still no sound to be heard in the room. Then, to my horror, the girl rushed around the table, a white napkin clutched in her hand, and twisted it around the neck of the young man. Her face contorted with fury, the woman strangled the man to death.

I screamed, dropped the candelabra, and covered my eyes, but only for a moment. I was afraid the ghost of the woman would come after me next, and I wanted to be ready for her. When I looked again, the young man lay dead on the floor, the young woman standing over him, clutching her hands together as if she could not believe what she had just done. Her hands were suddenly covered with blood, although no blood had been spilled. She looked disbelievingly at her hands and tried to rub them clean on her dress. No matter how hard she rubbed, the blood still stained her hands. Silently, she began to weep and wail, rubbing and rubbing at her hands.

There was a commotion in the hall, and the door burst open behind me. My parents and Mr. and Mrs. Jacques came running into the room. They stopped when they saw the ghost, who gave one last, silent wail and then disappeared. I gave a not-so-silent wail and ran to my Mama, weeping. Suddenly, I didn't feel so grown-up, and I never wanted to set foot in that mansion again.

"I am so sorry, Matilda," Mrs. Jacques cried as my parents bundled me up into my cloak and rushed me to the door.

"It is my own fault," Mama said. "If I had told Elizabeth the truth about this house, she wouldn't have gone looking for it by herself. I think we have all learned a lesson."

My parents took me home, and Mama tucked me into bed and told me the whole story. It was even more gruesome than I had imagined. The pretty young woman I had seen in the dining room was a French coquette whom the devil himself had taken as his mistress. The devil had bought her the mansion on St. Charles Avenue and lived with her there. But the devil was very busy with his devilish concerns, and he was away most of the time. The French girl grew lonely, and she took a dashing young Creole man as her lover.

The devil was fond of his mistress, and he was very jealous when he discovered she had another lover. He waited for the young man one night, leaning against a post outside on the street. When the young man emerged from the mansion, the devil approached him and told the young man that he had stolen the mistress of the devil himself. The young man was terrified. But the devil, having decided to discard his unfaithful mistress, told the young man he did not want her anymore. The devil offered the young man a million pounds if he would take the young woman and go far away. The only condition the devil made was that the young man and woman must adopt the names Monsieur and Madame L. The young man agreed to do as the devil said.

The next night, the couple had dinner together. As they ate, the young man told the woman about his conversation with the devil and the condition they had agreed upon. The young woman was furious when she heard the condition, realizing that the "L" stood for Lucifer, and that they would be forever branded wherever they went. Enraged, she rushed at her lover and strangled him with her napkin. When the young man lay dead at her feet, the devil appeared and killed her. Then the devil took the bodies of the young man and his mistress up to the rooftop. The moon was full that night, and the whole city could see the devil standing on the roof of the mansion as he skinned the young man and woman and devoured their remains.

The devil took the skin of the two unfortunate lovers and threw it to the ground to be eaten by the stray cats that wandered the streets at night. But when the devil tried to leave the roof of the mansion, he found that his head had been permanently attached to the roof's gable. In his jealous rage, the devil had forgotten that the Lord had ordered him not to work in the light of the full moon. As punishment for breaking the ban, the Lord had gathered up the skin of the humans that the devil had tossed upon the ground and had used it to bind the devil's head to the gable.

Every night thereafter, the ghosts of the devil's victims would appear in the dining room of the mansion and reenact the murder. The blood on the Frenchwoman's hands represented the eternal guilt she felt for killing her lover, a guilt that she could not rub out, no matter how many times she tried to clean her hands.

I was shaking violently by the time Mama finished the story.

"I wish I had never gone there," I cried. "I wish I had never heard that story."

Mama was a very wise woman. She didn't tell me it was my own fault for wandering where I was not supposed to go, she just hugged me and comforted me until I was calm enough to sleep.

I had nightmares about the ghosts for months afterward, and I would never let the coachman drive down St. Charles Avenue when I was in the carriage. I wondered how Mrs. Jacques could live in a house with such a horrible history and with such terrible ghosts. I didn't have to wonder long. The Jacqueses moved out of the house not long after my encounter with the ghosts, and the devil's mansion remained unoccupied until 1930, when it was finally demolished.

33

Chicky-licky-chow-chow-chow

MARYVILLE, TENNESSEE

It was Pop's idea to go and get some meat that day. I'd just finished feeding the hens when he shouted out, "Boy! Let's go get some beef."

That sounded all right by me. I was tired of eating rabbit, though my Ma could do some marvelous things with them.

So Pop and I set out for Maryville. It took us a couple of hours to get there, and then Pop had a jaw with some of his friends while I raced about with some of mine, and before you know it the day was nearly gone and we still hadn't gotten our beef. So Pop hurried over to the market and got us a side of beef complete with the head. That beef looked mighty good to me. My stomach was rumbling something fierce as we set off down the road toward home. Pop must have been thinking the same thing, because after an hour of walking, he set that beef down under a tree next to a creek and said to me, "Boy, this looks like a good spot to stop a while and cook some of this beef."

"Sounds good, Pop. But what are we going to do about a fire?" I asked. "Did you bring your flint?"

"Nope. I plumb forgot it in the rush to get on the road this morning," Pop said sheepishly.

CHICKY-LICKY-CHOW-CHOW-CHOW

I tried not to look too disappointed, but Pop must have heard my stomach growling because he grabbed two sticks and rubbed them together, trying to get a spark. I turned away, not wanting him to see how hungry I was. Then I saw a light at the top of one of the trees. It looked like the tree had caught fire, but as I watched for a moment, wondering if we should run before we were burned to death, I realized that the fire was only on one branch and wasn't burning anything. It looked sort of like a square-shaped man, the kind you might see on a totem pole, with spikes of flame sticking out all over it, like the quills of a porcupine.

"Pop, look at that," I said, pointing up at the crazy thing. My Pop turned around and looked up.

"Well, I'll be d—," Pop paused and looked sheepish again. Ma never let him swear in front of us kids. "That is, why don't you see if you can't get some of that fire, son, so we can roast some of this beef."

I nodded enthusiastically and swarmed up the tree. I'm a champion tree climber. I was real curious about that thing up there, all fiery spikes. As I neared the top of the tree, I could feel the heat coming off it. Then the thing spoke to me. It had a voice like the hiss and crackle of a fire. The sound of its voice gave me goose bumps.

"What do you want with me?" the thing asked. This was a bit tricky. I couldn't very well ask the thing for one of its fire quills.

"Pop said to come down and have some beef," I improvised. The thing considered this for a moment.

"Very well," the thing said. "I will come down for a while."

I slid down the tree as fast as I could. For some reason, the thing was making me nervous. I was sorry I had spoken to it, but it was too late to do anything about it now. I could feel the heat pouring off the thing as it followed me to the ground. Then the thing went immediately over to where my Pop was standing. It had a rolling gait and swayed a little as it approached him.

"Where is my beef?" the thing asked my Pop. Pop must have heard our conversation in the tree, because he had the head and skin all ready for the thing. I could hear that beef sizzle as the thing devoured it in a couple of bites. The rest of the beef was smoking in the heat coming from the fiery spikes that covered the thing. It smelled delicious, and I was really hankering for a bite of it myself when the thing gave a grunt and said to Pop, "More. I want more."

I could tell Pop was just as scared of the thing as I was because he gave the thing more without hesitation. As the thing ate the beef, Pop managed to cut off a few slices for us. By this time the meat was well done. I swallowed fast, and was sure glad I had, because the thing said, "Is this all you allow me, old man?"

Something about the hiss and sizzle of its voice made me break out into a cold sweat, in spite of the heat filling the clearing from those fiery quills. Pop gave it the rest of the beef.

When the thing finished the beef, it let out a tremendous burp and said, "More."

"That is all we have," Pop said bravely. He was sweating too, and I could tell from the sound of his voice that he wanted to get us out of this clearing as quick as he could. "We will have to go and get more."

The thing did not like this. Its fiery spikes began to wave about and grow hotter. I had to back up a few feet to keep from getting burned. "You will let your little boy stay with me until you return," the thing said finally. My Pop did not like this one bit.

"Ben must come with me," he said firmly. "I need him to drive the cow back here."

The thing frowned fiercely at us, but it finally let us leave. We took off lickety-split, hurrying back the way we had come. It was getting dark, and we didn't want to be on the road with that thing loose. Pop's plan was to stay the night with one of the people along the road and then travel a different way home in the morning.

We stopped at the first farmhouse and asked if we could spend the night. I'd seen the man once or twice before in town. He knew Pop by name and welcomed us into his house. The family had already finished their dinner, but the wife very kindly prepared a plate for each of us. Pop and I were still eating when we heard the noise. It sounded like the whoosh of a great wind, but within it was the crackling sound of flames. I froze, the fork halfway to my mouth, and stared across the table at Pop. Now we could hear footsteps shaking the ground. And a voice like the hiss of flames cried out, "Bum, bum, Sally Lum, tearing down trees and throwing them as I come." This was followed by the crash of a great tree falling to the ground.

"What is that?!" cried the head of the house. Pop wiped his mouth with shaking hands.

"Something is after me and the boy," he said reluctantly. The man and his wife stared at me and Pop for a long moment as the sound grew nearer.

"I don't think you can stay," said the man, taking his wife by the hand. "If it was just me . . . " His voice trailed off. Pop nodded at once. He wouldn't want that thing coming anywhere near Ma or the kids, and neither would I.

We hurried out the back door. I looked over my shoulder once as we raced across the back field of the farm. A light was coming through the dark trees toward us. It steered away from the farmhouse and headed toward the field, as if it could see where we were going. The thing was much taller now, and I could see some of its fiery spikes through the trees. I ran after Pop as fast as I could. "Bum, bum, Sally Lum," I heard the thing chanting as we jumped a fence and zigzagged back toward the road.

Pop must have had a destination in mind, for he turned left abruptly, back into the trees, and soon I saw a cabin ahead of us. Pop knocked on the door and an old trapper answered. Pop was just explaining that we needed a place to stay when the forest behind us began to glow as a familiar rushing, crackling wind sound filled the clearing. Above the noise, I could hear the thing chanting, "Bum, bum, Sally Lum, tearing down trees and throwing them as I come."

The trapper turned pale and slammed the door in Pop's face. Pop was looking pretty grim now. He grabbed me by the hand and yanked me through the trees. I was so tired I was shaking, but I wouldn't stop for anything. That thing was coming for us, and I didn't want to find out what would happen when it caught us.

Pop stopped at two or three more houses on the road, but no one would take us in. The people in the last house wouldn't even open the door. They just shouted at us to go away. No matter how fast we ran, we could always hear the rushing, crackling sound. If we paused for too long, we could see the light moving through the darkness toward us. I was trembling with exhaustion, and crying, but I couldn't help myself. I kept imagining what it would be like to burn to death. And all the time I could hear faintly, in the distance, "Bum, bum, Sally Lum, tearing down trees and throwing them as I come."

Pop had to pick me up and carry me as he ran down the road. Town had never seemed so far away as it did now. But even if we reached it, what if no one would take us in? Pop stumbled over a rut in the road and fell to his knees.

"Put me down, Pop. I can run," I lied. I knew it was too much for my old man to carry me and try to keep ahead of that thing.

"What's your problem?" a voice asked out of the darkness. I looked around. There was no one there, except a rabbit sitting by the road. Pop struggled to his feet with me still on his shoulder.

"Who's there?" Pop asked shakily.

"I am," said the rabbit. We both stared at it, shocked. Neither of us had ever heard of a talking rabbit. But then again, neither of us had ever seen a fiery thing before either. This seemed to be a day of strange happenings.

Pop must have come to the same conclusion. "We need help," Pop said to the rabbit. "We are being chased by a thing made of fire."

The rabbit nodded. "If you go into my house, I will protect you." The rabbit pointed one long ear toward the thicket behind it. Pop was desperate. He thanked the rabbit and put me down, and we crawled into the brush, leaving the rabbit sitting by the road.

The sound of the crackling wind grew louder, and the forest began to glow with an uncanny light. The earth shook with the sound of footsteps, and a hissing voice cried, "Bum, bum, Sally Lum, tearing down trees and throwing them as I come."

I was shaking all over. I clung to my Pop's hand like I used to when I was little and waited for the thing to come and burn me to death. After all, what could a little rabbit, even one that could talk, do to such a thing?

"Is that the thing that's chasing you?" the rabbit called to us from the road.

"Yes," Pop said. His voice trembled on the word, and I gripped his hand as tight as I could. I was angry at the thing for scaring my Pop.

"Stay where you are and I will protect you," said the rabbit.

The light grew and grew, and suddenly I could see the thing coming down the road toward the rabbit. The thing had grown twice as big as a man and the ground shook with its approach. The thing saw the rabbit and stopped.

"Have you seen a man and a boy pass this way?" the thing asked the rabbit.

"Chicky-licky-chow-chow-chow," said the rabbit, getting up and doing a little dance as it spoke.

The thing frowned fiercely.

"I said, have you seen a man and a boy pass this way?" the thing shouted.

"Chicky-licky-chow-chow-chow," said the rabbit, spinning around and wagging its long ears at the thing.

"Tell me, have you seen a man and a boy pass this way?!" the thing roared, its flame quills growing as long as tree branches. The heat was intense, worse than standing too close to the fireplace. The light from the thing was brighter than noon. I was afraid the thing might see us hiding in the brush, but it was too busy shouting at the rabbit. "Tell me what I want to know or I will swallow you!" the thing shouted.

"Chicky-licky-chow-chow-chow," sang the rabbit. It jumped up on the thing's leg and leapt from there to its top. The rabbit danced a little jig, repeating, "Chicky-licky-chow-chow-chow. Chicky-licky-chow-chow-chow. Once I had a summer house, now I've got a winter house."

"I am going to butt your brains out against a tree!" roared the thing, infuriated by the rabbit's song and dance. The rabbit just laughed and said, "Chicky-licky-chow-chow-chow."

So, the thing reared back, aimed itself at a giant pine tree, and butted itself against the thick trunk. At the last moment, the rabbit leapt clear, as the thing hit the tree. The thing burst open, and it dropped dead onto the ground, all its flames extinguishing at once. The ground shook under the impact of the thing's fall, but in the sudden darkness, I couldn't see what had happened to the rabbit. Had it been crushed by the thing when it fell? Then I heard the soft thump of rabbit paws on the road and heard a cheerful voice singing, "Chicky-licky-chow-chow-chow."

Pop crawled out of the thicket and pulled me after him. We crouched by the brush, our eyes adjusting to the darkness. The moon had risen, and as my eyes adjusted, I saw the thing on our right. It seemed to be sinking into the earth. As I watched, it disappeared completely and the ground closed over it.

The rabbit appeared right in front of us and Pop said simply, "Thank you."

"You're welcome," said the rabbit gravely. It winked one eye, danced a little jig and sang, "Chicky-licky-chow-chow-chow." Then we were alone in the moonlight.

Pop never shot another rabbit as long as he lived. And neither of us was ever particularly fond of beef again.

34

The Lady

RICHMOND, VIRGINIA

"If only . . . " The phrase came frequently to the lips of the good Doctor and his Wife. If only they had time and energy. If only they had money. If only they had assistance. But they had none of these things. For themselves, they asked for little, but for their children they wanted everything. It shamed the Doctor and his wife that they had nothing to give their children; not even an education.

The Doctor was severely injured in the Civil War and had walked with a limp since the second battle of Manassas. This injury kept him from doing a full day of physician rounds, and it made his life a misery when he was called out to a birth in the middle of the night. On his dear wife fell the burden of keeping house and home up-and-running; itself an awesome task. The couple had no money to hire help, since the residents of post-war Virginia could only pay the good Doctor in food and clothing. Without money, they couldn't afford the luxury of hiring a tutor for their intelligent sons or a music teacher for their gifted daughter. And the children—who worked as hard as their parents to make ends meet—were so sleepy at night that

THE LADY

they often fell asleep before the Doctor or his wife could spare time to give them a lesson.

The Doctor and his wife were rehashing the issue of their children's education one evening as a mighty storm raged over the countryside. The Doctor's injured hip ached with the cold and humidity and he huddled next to the warmth of the fire, too tired to rise and go to bed. As his good wife knitted and fretted beside him, there came a faint knock on the front door.

"Oh no," moaned the wife. "Not tonight. You are too sore and weary to go out, my dear husband."

"You know that I took oath to answer the summons of those in need," the Doctor replied gently, using both hands to push himself out of the chair. He grabbed his wife's arm for support as he limped toward the door.

The couple opened the door together, and staggered backward as wind and rain whipped inside, almost knocking them over. At first, their fire-dazzled eyes perceived nothing but darkness. Then the wife looked down and saw a woman lying in a pathetic, soaking wet heap at their feet. The Doctor picked the woman up and carried her to the fire, while his wife pushed the door shut with much effort against the wind.

The woman was far gone with cold and fatigue. The Doctor dried her off and wrapped her in warm blankets; all the while speculating on whom this stranger might be. The Doctor knew every man, woman and child for nearly fifty miles, but he had never seen this woman before. She was unnaturally pale, as if she spent all of her waking life indoors, and her wrists were red and swollen as if the cuffs of her tight sleeves—now mere rags— had cut off her circulation. The Doctor bound the strange wrist injuries while his wife administered a stimulant.

When the Lady roused at last, her eyes focused first upon the library which lined the walls of the Doctor's small parlor. "Books," she murmured. "Books! It has been so long . . . " She closed her eyes weakly, but there was a smile upon her face.

"Shh," said the Wife, smoothing back her tangled hair. "You can read your fill tomorrow. Tonight, you must rest."

The Lady fell into a deep sleep and they put her on the bed in the tiny spare room that the Doctor used as his office. Then they went upstairs to their own room for the night.

The morning after the storm dawned glorious and fair. The Doctor's wife lingered over her milking; enjoying the sights and smells of a world washed clean. As she carried her pails toward the house, she heard an angelic voice singing her favorite song, accompanied by the long disused parlor piano.

"Sweet Amaryllis, by a spring's sweet side . . . " trilled the lovely soprano. The wife beamed, recognizing her daughter Virginia's voice. But who was playing the piano?

The wife hurried inside just as the Virginia's song broke off. A sweet contralto commanded: "Sing the line again with a full breath, Virginia. Do not break the phrase in the middle." The pale Lady spoke from her seat on the piano bench. Her pale hands, ringed by bandages, lay upon the keys.

Seeing the Doctor's wife in the doorway, the Lady added: "Madam, your daughter has great talent and may be one of the Great Singers of the world if she is properly trained."

Opposite her, the Doctor and his two sons stood listening in the door to the kitchen, faces beaming with delight.

"Can you teach her, Lady?" asked the Doctor.

The Lady's eyes traveled from the radiant Virginia to the eager faces of the two boys.

"I can teach them all, Sir," she replied.

And teach them she did; with skill and authority and the simple magic possessed by the greatest teachers which calls forth the very best from the minds under their tutelage. The children soaked in their instruction and studied harder than they ever had before, striving to please the Lady they loved.

The Lady never told the family her name. After the first inquiry they did not ask again, assuming she had run away from a cruel husband or father and needed a place of refuge. It did not bother them; for she was their Lady, the children's beloved governess, come to the Doctor's family to fulfill their great need.

For five years, the Lady strove mightily to educate the Doctor's family, until both boys had qualified for university and Virginia had learned all she could teach and could sing sweetly in 3 languages. Early one evening, as a great storm rolled into valley, the children's governess looked one last time upon her sleeping charges, knowing she had done everything she could to ready them for the wide world. Then she slipped away—as she had first come—during the lashing winds and thunderous rains of the storm.

The Doctor and his family wore themselves to the bone searching for their beloved Lady, to no avail. She was gone as a mist, not to be seen again. "Perhaps she was an angel, sent to minister to us in our time of need," the wife said to her family and friends. "God works in mysterious ways."

Soon the children were grown and flown; the boys to university and Virginia on a classical music tour that spanned three continents. Of all the songs the great singer performed, the best loved was the old Southern ballad called Sweet

Amaryllis. Virginia wept whenever she sang it, remembering her beloved Lady.

The Doctor had prospered in the years following the disappearance of the Lady. Once his children were grown he turned more and more to charitable works and the donation of his professional time to those in need. One morning, the Doctor paid a visit to an infamous Asylum for the Insane. The Asylum superintendent herself took him on a tour of the facilities. They walked through the narrow hallways, accompanied for safety by two husky orderlies, discussing public heath improvements and the best ways to treat the medically insane.

As the group turned into the corridor that housed the more violent patients, the Doctor heard a sweet contralto voice singing Sweet Amaryllis. The Doctor stopped abruptly before the barred door from which the voice emerged and asked the matron about the inmate.

"An interesting case," the superintendent said. "She was left upon our doorstep one night many years ago—before my time— bound hand and foot to keep her from committing violence against herself and others. After several years in the asylum, she broke out of her shackles and vanished; only to reappear five years later and beg to be readmitted. She was afraid she would hurt someone in her madness."

"What is her name?" the Doctor asked.

"We never knew her name. We just call her the Lady. Sometimes the Lady can be very gentle, but in my experience the gentle ones are the worst kind. You never know when they might lash out. Don't you agree doctor?"

Behind the door, the song broke off abruptly in a sob that broke the good Doctor's heart. "Open this door," he commanded to the orderlies.

The superintendent looked alarmed. "Doctor, be careful. The Lady is extremely dangerous."

As the door swung open, the Doctor saw a familiar pale form standing in the middle of the room. Loose chains bound the Lady to the wall. Her wrists, under the shackles, were swollen and red. The wounds were the same as those the Doctor had bandaged five years before. The Lady's eyes were closed, and she swayed as she hummed a few more bars of Sweet Amaryllis.

"Remove those shackles," the Doctor commanded, stepping briskly toward his former governess.

The Lady's eyes flew open, and the Doctor found himself gazing into pupils glowing red with insane hatred and a lust to kill. He stopped in his tracks, stunned by the evil menace twisting the beloved countenance. In that frozen moment, the Lady sprang to the full length of her chains, her long fingernails clawing at the Doctor's face. He fell to the floor, blood streaming from both eyes and the Lady laughed maniacally as she stood in triumph over her latest victim.

The husky orderlies leapt into the room and wrestled the Lady down onto the bed while the superintendent dragged the Doctor to safety. But it was too late to save him. The Doctor's eyes were permanently damaged by Lady's blow. He never saw again.

35

Wiley and the Hairy Man

TOMBIGBEE REGION, ALABAMA

Wiley's papa was just about the laziest, no-account man in Alabama. He never did a lick of work, letting the weeds grow till they were higher than the cotton, stealing the neighbors' vegetables on dark nights, and robbing corpses before they could be buried. Everyone hereabouts knew that Wiley's papa was never gonna cross the river Jordan. No, sir! The Hairy Man would come for him, and he'd never get to heaven.

Well, Wiley's papa fell off the ferry one day, and everyone reckoned the Hairy Man must have gotten him because they never found the body. They checked up and down the river and in the still pools by the sandbanks, but there was no sign of him. While they were checking the fast waters downstream, they heard a gruff laugh coming from the far bank, and they knew it was the Hairy Man. That's when they stopped looking for Wiley's papa.

Wiley's mama was a smart woman who knew lots about conjuring because she came from the swamps of Tombigbee. She told Wiley that the Hairy Man was gonna come for him too, since he'd already gotten Wiley's papa.

"So you'd best keep a careful look about you."

WILEY AND THE HAIRY MAN

"I'll be careful, Mama," Wiley promised. "I'm gonna keep my hound dogs with me all the time, just like you taught me."

"That's right. The Hairy Man doesn't like hound dogs," said Wiley's mama.

So Wiley was right careful to keep the hounds with him when he did his chores. But one day, as Wiley was chopping down some poles in the swamp to use for a hen roost, a stoat went running right past his hound dogs. The dogs jumped up mighty quick and chased that stoat clean across the swamp and off into the woods. They ran a long way down the river, until Wiley couldn't hear them yelping any more.

But Wiley could hear something stomp, stomp, stomping through the trees—and he knew it was the Hairy Man. He looked up, and sure enough the Hairy Man was coming through the trees toward him. The Hairy Man was as ugly as sin, with hair all over his body, and eyes that burned like fire. The Hairy Man was grinning and drooling all over his big teeth, and Wiley didn't like the looks of him one bit.

"Don't you be a lookin' at me like that," Wiley said to the Hairy Man, dropping his ax and climbing a big bay tree that was nearby. He figured the Hairy Man couldn't climb the tree because his feet looked like cows' feet, and Wiley hadn't ever seen a cow up a tree.

"Now what'd you climb up there for, Wiley?" asked the Hairy Man.

Wiley kept climbing higher as the Hairy Man stopped at the bottom of the tree. The Hairy Man sure was ugly. Wiley didn't like the looks of him one bit and didn't stop climbing until he reached the top of the tree.

"How come you're climbing trees?" asked the Hairy Man again.

"My mama told me to stay away from you, and that's what I aim to do," Wiley said, wishing that the tree would grow faster.

Wiley noticed that the Hairy Man was carrying a sack over his shoulder. He didn't like the look of that sack any more than he liked the look of the Hairy Man. "What you got in that sack?"

"There ain't nothing in my sack . . . yet." The Hairy Man grinned up at Wiley and seized Wiley's ax.

"Get out of here!" shouted Wiley.

"Ha!" retorted the Hairy Man as he began chopping down the bay tree.

Wiley was plumb scared. He held on tight to the tree and tried to remember what his mama had taught him about conjuring. There must be something he could do. Then he remembered a chant his mama had taught him.

"Fly chips, fly. Go back to yer place," Wiley shouted. The wood chips flew back into the tree and sealed the hole the Hairy Man had made with the ax. The Hairy Man cursed and shouted and started chopping faster. Wiley knew he was in trouble, but he chanted faster and faster. The wood chips flew in and out, in and out of the bay tree, but soon they were flying more out than in. The Hairy Man was bigger and stronger than Wiley, and he was gaining on the boy.

Wiley's voice was getting hoarse from all that chanting, and he was mighty afraid. Then he heard a faint yelping from far away. His hound dogs were coming back. Wiley drew in a deep breath and shouted, "Here dogs! Here dogs!" Then he kept chanting the spell, "Fly chips, fly. Go back to yer place."

The Hairy Man laughed. "You ain't got no dogs. I sent a shoat to draw them away from you."

But Wiley shouted for the dogs again, and this time the Hairy Man heard them yelping too. The Hairy Man looked worried.

"I'll teach you to conjure if you come down," he tried to bargain with Wiley.

"My mama can conjure, and she'll teach me all I want to know," Wiley said.

Enraged, the Hairy Man cursed and stomped his cow feet. Wiley and the Hairy Man could hear the dogs getting closer and closer. The Hairy Man shouted one more curse word, threw down the ax, and ran off into the woods.

As soon as Wiley got home, he told his mama all about how the Hairy Man almost got him.

"Did he have his sack?" asked Wiley's mama.

"Yes, ma'am."

"He's gonna come after you again, Wiley," said Wiley's mama. "Next time he comes, don't you be climbing no bay trees."

"I won't, Mama. They ain't big enough."

"Don't you be climbing no tree at all," Wiley's mama said.

"What should I do then?" asked Wiley.

Wiley's mama told him how to trick the Hairy Man so he could get away. Wiley listened carefully.

"I dunno, Mama. It just don't seem right," Wiley worried. But he promised to do what his mama said.

The next day, Wiley tied up his hound dogs before he went down to the swamp to finish making his hen roost. It wasn't too long before he heard a stamp, stamp, stamping sound coming from the woods. Wiley looked up, and sure enough, there was the Hairy Man coming through the trees, grinning and drooling all over his big teeth. The Hairy Man knew the hound dogs were tied up at the house more than a mile away. He was carrying the sack over his shoulder again, and Wiley wanted to climb another tree to get away. But Wiley stayed where he was, remembering the promise he'd made to his mama.

"Hello, Hairy Man," he said, just as his mama had told him to.

"Hello, Wiley," said the Hairy Man, taking the sack off his shoulder and opening it up.

"Hairy Man, I hear you're the best conjurer in the world," said Wiley quickly.

"You heard right," said the Hairy Man.

"I bet you can't turn yourself into a giraffe," Wiley said.

"That's an easy one," said the Hairy Man, and he turned himself into a giraffe lickety-split.

"Bet you can't turn yourself into an alligator," said Wiley. The giraffe turned and twisted and became an alligator, but it kept its eye on Wiley the whole time it was transforming, to make sure he didn't run away.

"Well, that's pretty good. But just about anybody can turn into something as big as a man. It takes a mighty strong conjurer to turn into something small, like a possum."

"Ha!" said the alligator, twisting and turning itself around until it turned into a possum. Quick as a wink, Wiley grabbed the possum, tied it up tight in the sack, and threw it in the river. Then he started home through the swamp. But he was only halfway there when the Hairy Man came walking toward him through the woods. Wiley yelped in horror and climbed up high into a tree.

"I turned myself into a wind and blew my way out of that sack," said the Hairy Man proudly as he came up to Wiley's tree. "Now I'm gonna sit here till you get so hungry you fall out of the tree."

Wiley didn't know what to do. His hound dogs were still tied up a mile away. The Hairy Man sat with his back against the tree and said, "You still want to see me conjure?"

Wiley had an idea. "Well," he said. "You did some pretty fancy tricks, Hairy Man. But I bet you can't make things disappear, so nobody knows where they go."

"Huh," the Hairy Man snorted. "That's what I do best. See that old bird's nest? Now look—it's gone."

"How am I to know it was there in the first place? Bet you can't make something I know about disappear!"

"Ha! Look at your shirt," said the Hairy Man. Wiley's shirt had disappeared. Wiley kept his face serious. He didn't want the Hairy Man to know what he was up to.

"That's just an old shirt. This old rope I got tying up my britches is conjured. You can't make something conjured disappear, Hairy Man."

The Hairy Man was mad clean through at Wiley's tone. "I can make all the rope in the whole county disappear," he shouted.

"Ha, ha," Wiley laughed scornfully.

The Hairy Man jumped up and yelled, "All the rope in this county—disappear!"

Wiley made a quick grab for his pants as the rope holding them up disappeared. Then he yelled for his hound dogs; the rope he'd tied them up with had disappeared too. They came yelping and barking, and the Hairy Man ran off, mad because Wiley had tricked him again.

As soon as Wiley got home, his mama asked him if he put the Hairy Man in the sack like she told him.

"Yes, ma'am, but he turned himself into wind and blew himself out again. Then he trapped me up a tree."

Wiley told her how he tricked the Hairy Man so he could escape.

"Wiley, you fooled that Hairy Man twice," said his mama. "If you can fool him once more, he'll leave you alone for the rest of your days. But he's mighty hard to fool a third time."

"We've gotta think of something, Mama."

Wiley's mama sat down next to the fire, and she thought and thought. Wiley wanted to think too, but he knew he had to protect them from the Hairy Man first. So, he tied one dog to each door and put the broom and the ax over the window so they'd fall down if anyone tried to open it from the outside. Then he built a big fire in the fireplace so anyone trying to come down the chimney would be burned.

By the time Wiley had finished protecting the house, his mama had thought up something.

"Wiley," she said, "go fetch me the little suckling pig we have in the pen with that old sow."

So, Wiley went down and caught the suckling pig, leaving the old sow squealing indignantly in the pen. He gave the little pig to his mama, who stuck the pig in Wiley's bed.

"Now hide yourself in the loft and don't come down no matter what," Wiley's mama told him. So, Wiley went and hid in the loft. It wasn't too long before the wind started to howl outside, and the trees started shaking, and the hound dogs began to growl. Wiley looked out through a crack in the wall and saw the hound dog by the front door watching something in the woods. It started to snarl as a horned animal the size of a donkey went running past. The hound dog barked something fierce and tried to break free, but he couldn't get loose. When a second animal came running from the woods, the hound got loose and chased it far away into the swamp. Wiley hurried to the other side of the loft to look out at the back door. The rope that Wiley had used to tie his other dog was broken too, and Wiley could see the hound chasing something that looked like a large possum into the trees.

"The Hairy Man must be on his way," Wiley muttered. And sure enough, Wiley heard a stomp, stomp, stomping noise coming from the trees. Then Wiley heard the sound of feet up on the roof of the house. The Hairy Man started to swear. He'd touched the chimney, hot from the big fire Wiley had made in the fireplace. So the Hairy Man jumped off the roof, walked right up to the house, and knocked on the front door.

"Mama, I've come to take your baby," the Hairy Man shouted. "I got your man, and I want your baby."

"You ain't gonna get him, nohow!" Mama shouted back.

"I sure will, Mama. I'm gonna bite you till you give him to me. I got blue gums, Mama, and my bite is poisonous as a cottonmouth's."

"I got poisoned gums of my own, Hairy Man," Mama said.

"I'll set your house afire with a lightning bolt," the Hairy Man threatened.

"I'll put it out with sweet milk," Mama retorted.

"Mama, I'm gonna dry up your spring and send a million boll weevils to eat up your cotton and make your cow go dry if you don't give me your baby."

"Hairy Man, you ain't gonna do that. That's just mean."

"I'm a mean man," said the Hairy Man. "There ain't no man alive that's as mean as me. Now give me your baby."

"If I give you my baby, you gonna leave everything else alone and go right away from here?" asked Mama.

"I swear that's what I'll do," said the Hairy Man.

So, Mama opened the front door and let the Hairy Man in.

"He's over in that bed," said Mama. The Hairy Man ran over to the bed and snatched the covers away.

"Hey!" he shouted. "There ain't nothin' in here but a suckling pig."

"I never said what kind of baby I was giving you," said Mama. "And that suckling pig was mine to give, before I promised it to you."

The Hairy Man had been tricked for the third time and he knew it. He stomped and yelled and swore and knocked over all the furniture. Then he grabbed up the baby pig and ran out into the swamp, knocking trees over in his rage. The Hairy Man tore a path through the swamp that looked like a cyclone had set down right next to the house.

When the Hairy Man was gone, Wiley came down from the loft.

"Is that Hairy Man gone for good, Mama?"

"He's gone for good," Mama said. "That Hairy Man can't ever hurt you again because we fooled him three times."

Wiley gave his mama a big hug, then they got out the last of his papa's moonshine that they had been saving for a special occasion and celebrated long into the night.

36

Spanish Moss

DAYTONA BEACH, FLORIDA

It was early fall when the captain and his men made camp on the coast, planning to hunt and fish for a week to supplement their meager supplies with fresh meat. Their regiment was charged with exploring and taming the wilds of this new land they had discovered, and they planned to march northward for many days.

Among the company was a beautiful Native American woman they had captured during a skirmish a few days previous. The Spanish soldiers had killed all their native attackers but had spared the life of the woman and had brought her along with them. In truth, they might have let her go had the captain not been smitten by her. She was tall and graceful, with masses of long dark hair and luminous dark eyes. He had never seen her equal for loveliness or spirit.

The captain tried to woo the beautiful captive as they journeyed northward, inviting her to dine in his tent, picking wildflowers for her, and reciting Spanish poetry to her. But the lovely captive spurned his advances and demanded that he release her so that she might return to her people. As his hopes of winning her love evaporated, the captain's infatuation turned

238

SPANISH MOSS

to hatred. He was furious at the woman's open defiance, afraid that it might undermine his standing among the troops.

The situation came to a head that evening. The woman was stirring the fire, and a long strand of her silky hair fell across her cheek. When the captain reached out and brushed it gently back behind her ear, the woman slapped his face, right in front of his men. Enraged, the captain struck her a fierce blow, sending her flying backward into the dirt. Leaping to his feet, he towered over the beautiful captive and swore he would cut off her head and put it on a pike by the entrance to his camp as a warning to any who defied him.

The woman raised her chin defiantly and said, "If you do this evil deed, I swear my spirit will follow you wherever you go!"

With an incoherent shout of rage, the captain drew his sword and slashed downward three times. The third cut severed the woman's head from her neck. Grabbing the head by its silky black hair, the captain strode to the edge of camp, blood dripping in his wake. He thrust a pike through the bottom of the head and buried the end of the pike in the ground so that the head could be seen by all his men. The woman's face was set in a look of defiance, even in death, and her long, silky hair twisted this way and that in the breeze. The captain marched back to his tent and got very drunk, and the men avoided him for the rest of the evening.

But in the morning, one of the officers came hurrying into the tent, his cheeks pale with fright. "Sir, the head . . . the woman . . . " he stuttered incoherently, unable to finish a sentence. The captain waved for him to continue, but he just beckoned mutely to his superior officer to follow him outside. As soon as he stepped foot out of the tent, the captain could see what had frightened the man. The woman's head atop the bloodstained pike was now standing right outside his tent. Overnight her long black hair had turned gray; her face was pointed directly toward his tent, her defiant dead eyes fixed upon its entrance.

The captain's heart thundered within him at the sight. "Is this someone's idea of a joke?" he roared, using anger to hide his fear.

"No, sir," the officer babbled. "The men swear that they did not touch it. They say it is the curse come true."

"I don't believe in curses," the captain snapped, cold sweat running down his back, despite his words. "Put the head back at the entrance to the camp, and tell the men that the first one who touches it will be severely punished!"

The captain stormed back into his tent. It was only when he was alone that he staggered into a chair, his knees trembling too much to keep him upright. What had he done?

During breakfast, his eyes moved more than once to the bloodstained pike at the entrance to the camp. As he finished his meal and rose to his feet, the pike suddenly vanished. The captain gasped and hurried forward, one step, two. He almost rammed into the head on the pike, which reappeared right in front of him, the woman's eyes gazing defiantly into his own, her long gray hair blowing wildly about the bloodstained pike, even though no wind was blowing. The captain screamed in terror, staggering backward with his hands in front of his face. He babbled a prayer aloud as his men came running. At the sight of the ghastly head on the pike, they retreated behind their captain.

"Take it down," the captain roared. "Take it down and bury it! Now!"

After a palpable hesitation, a few of the braver officers came forward to deal with the head on the pike. When it was gone, the captain staggered back into his tent and fell on his knees, vomiting his breakfast onto the ground. Mother of God, what was happening to him?

Taking long, slow breaths, the captain reminded himself that the woman was dead and that the curse of a native could not prevail over a good Catholic like himself. Could it?

He had cleaned himself up and donned a new uniform by the time his officers came to report that the head was buried deep beneath a stone. He nodded his thanks and started giving out the day's orders as if nothing had happened. And nothing did happen for the rest of the day. As they realized the haunting— or whatever it was—had ceased, the activity around the camp grew cheerful. They had foiled the curse of the native woman! She was dead and buried and would haunt them no longer. The captain went to sleep in good spirits. They would stay here for a week, he decided, before making their way northward. It would do the men good to have a rest.

He was awakened the next morning by a man's scream coming from the edge of camp. He was up and armed as soon as his eyes opened, prepared for an attack by the area natives. He ran outside and joined the other men racing toward the sound, swords drawn. At the edge of camp, they found an officer shivering from head to toe. When he saw his comrades in various stages of dress waving their swords, he pointed to the tree beneath which the woman's head had been buried. Hanging from the tree were long, silky gray strands blowing in the sea breeze. The captain gasped, shivers running up his arms and spine. It was her hair! The woman's hair!

Then the man nearest the officer, who was a bit of a daredevil, stepped forward and grabbed the hair off the tree. "It's moss, you fool!" he said. "Just moss!"

Just moss, the captain repeated to himself. But it was unlike any moss he had ever seen before—not on this island, not in Florida, not anywhere in the Spanish empire. And it looked just like her hair . . .

"I've had enough of this nonsense," the captain said aloud. "Break camp. We're heading north!"

"Yes, sir," his men replied. With many a backward glance toward the moss now lying on the ground, the soldiers hurried away to do as he ordered. When they were gone, the captain buried the moss in the earth under the tree. They would leave this cursed place and travel north to fulfill their mission.

The captain didn't relax until they had marched many miles to the north. Just to be safe, he inspected the trees around the clearing where they made camp that night. There was no sign of any long-haired moss growing upon them. Good.

The captain slept soundly that night, undisturbed by the rising wind that came in from the sea. He was the first one up in the morning. As he stepped out into the grove of trees, his eyes were caught by long, gray strands growing from every branch. The trees were covered with hair! No, not hair, moss, he corrected himself. But he remembered the native woman's curse: "If you do this evil deed, I swear my spirit will follow you wherever you go!" And the moss had followed him up the coast. He stood frozen to the spot as his men awakened around him. One by one, they came to stare at the moss-trimmed trees.

The moss blew frantically back and forth in a breeze they could not feel. And the captain could sense the dead woman's gaze upon him, though her head was buried far away.

"Let's go," he snapped, finally breaking the uncanny silence. Without a word, his men broke camp, and they hurried away without pausing to eat. The captain could feel the eyes of his men on his back as they marched, though none dared speak of what they had seen.

They paused at midday to break their fast. While they ate, the captain could see the bare trees growing moss. It slithered down the trunks and slid up and over branches, gray and silky and waving in a nonexistent breeze. The troop hurried through their meal and almost ran out of the clearing. As they marched northward, the moss followed them. The few times he glanced over his shoulder, the captain saw moss growing over the bare trees in their wake. He felt sick to his stomach, and it was only the force of his iron will that kept his meal down.

Grimly they continued their journey. A breeze sprang up from the sea, and on the breeze was a familiar voice—a woman's voice. "I will follow you," it whispered in the captain's ear. "I will follow you."

They only stopped marching when sheer darkness forced them to pause. They camped on the beach well away from the trees, and the men built a huge bonfire. Only the captain's tent was erected that night, and he went into it reluctantly, still hearing a voice on the breeze. Or was it only in his head?

When the captain did not emerge from his tent the next morning, the officers went inside to check on him. His bed was rumpled but empty. Alarmed, they hurried outside and began searching the beach for their commander. And then they saw a figure dangling from a gnarled oak at the edge of the beach. The men hurried toward it and saw their captain hanging by the neck from a thickly tangled skein of gray moss. The moss had strangled the life out of him and was growing all over his dangling body.

The men stared at the moss-covered figure in terror. Finally, the daredevil soldier cut him down. The officers ordered camp broken down, and the troop retreated south toward St. Augustine, abandoning all pretext of obeying orders now that their commander was dead. They stayed as close to the shore as they could, trying to avoid the trees. The moss followed them.

When the company broke up in St. Augustine, the soldiers were reassigned to other units and sent many places around the world. Wherever a soldier from that ill-fated unit journeyed, the moss followed him. In time the newly christened "Spanish" moss covered the whole South; a silent witness to injustice revenged.

37

West Hell

JACKSONVILLE, FLORIDA

Now Big John de Conqueror was just about the holiest man that ever lived. Everybody in Florida loved Big John, and the animals, well, they did too. Big John would fly on an eagle's back to many places us regular folks couldn't go, and he saw many strange things and met many strange creatures.

Big John was just about the happiest man that ever lived too, only he didn't have a wife, and he wanted one. So whenever he flew out on his eagle, Big John kept a lookout for a nice girl that he could love and marry.

One day, Big John was taking a trip down to Hell to make sure everything was working properly down there. As he was flying over Regular Hell, he caught a glimpse of the devil's beautiful girl-child. Well, Big John de Conqueror, he fell in love with the devil's daughter lickety-split. He landed his eagle near her and they talked for hours. The devil's daughter, she loved Big John right back. So Big John asked her to marry him, and she agreed. They were going to elope, because there was no way the devil would agree to his daughter marrying Big John. But the eagle was only big enough to hold Big John, so they decided to

WEST HELL

take the devil's famous pair of horses, Hallowed-Be-Thy-Name and Thy-Kingdom-Come.

Well, Big John got up on Hallowed-Be-Thy-Name, and the devil's daughter jumped up on the back of Thy-Kingdom-Come, and they rode those horses up toward Earth. But one of the imps told the devil what was happening, and faster than lightning the devil leaped on his famous jumping bull and pursued Big John and his daughter.

The devil's daughter looked back and shouted to Big John de Conqueror, "My daddy's coming! What should we do?"

Big John turned Hallowed-Be-Thy-Name toward West Hell and cried, "This way!"

But the devil's daughter stopped Thy-Kingdom-Come. Big John turned to look at her and saw that she was shaking with fear. "Oh, Big John," said she, "I am afraid to go to West Hell. My daddy won't even let the imps go in there because it's so hot and tough and only the worst sinners stay there."

Big John rode back and took her hand. "I will protect you," he said to the devil's daughter. She saw the goodness shining out of Big John de Conqueror and agreed to ride through West Hell with him. They could both hear the devil getting closer, his jumping bull roaring angrily, so they rode as fast as they could. It got hotter and hotter as they hurried through West Hell, and some of the vile sinners tried to pull Big John and the devil's daughter off their horses so they could ride away from West Hell. But Big John was as strong as he was good, and he chased them off.

But the devil caught up with the couple before they reached the end of West Hell, and the devil and Big John started to fight. And what a wrestling match it was, what with Big John being so holy and the devil being so evil. Big John and the devil struggled and fought and wrestled and boxed. They rolled through pits of fire and scared the sinners so much that the sinners vowed to be as holy as the angels in the future if only the devil and Big John would just stop fighting. The devil's daughter was crying and shouting and encouraging Big John and shaming her father. And when Big John got ahold of the devil and tore off his arm and beat him with it until the devil surrendered, the devil's daughter shouted "Hallelujah!" with relief. Then, she gave Big John a kiss.

So Big John and the devil's daughter were married right then and there, while the devil grumbled and put his arm back on. And Big John passed out ice water to all the sinners in West Hell, who were so thankful that the fighting had stopped that they were all on their best behavior. Before Big John left with his bride, he turned the damper down in some parts of Hell and told the devil he would turn West Hell into an icehouse if the devil ever turned the heat back up.

Sometimes during winter, the parlor in Hell gets chilly, and the devil has to build a fire in the fireplace to keep warm. But the devil doesn't dare turn up the heat because Big John told the devil that he and his missus and his family won't come visit unless the devil keeps the heat down. And the devil knows Big John means it.

38

Raw Head

Way back in the deep woods there lived a scrawny old woman who had a reputation for being the best conjuring woman in the mountains. With her bedraggled black-and-gray hair and her crooked nose, Eliza Blake was not a pretty picture, but she was the best there was at fixing what ailed a man—and that was all that mattered.

Eliza Blake's house was full of herbs and roots and bottles filled with conjuring medicine. The walls were lined with strange books brimming with magical spells. Eliza Blake was the only one living in the Hollow who knew how to read; her granny, who was also a conjurer, had taught her the skill as part of her magical training.

The only friend Eliza Blake had was a mean old razorback hog that ran wild around her place. It rooted so much in her kitchen garbage that all the leftover spells started affecting it. Some folks swore up and down that the old razorback hog sometimes walked upright like a man. "Raw Head" was the name Eliza Blake gave the razorback, referring maybe to the way the ugly creature looked a bit like some of the dead pigs you could see come butchering time down in Hog-Scald Hollow.

RAW HEAD

The razorback didn't mind the funny name. Raw Head kept following Eliza Blake around her little cabin and rooting up the kitchen leftovers. He'd even walk to town with her when she went to the local mercantile to sell her home remedies.

Folks got so used to seeing Raw Head and Eliza Blake in the town that it looked mighty strange one day around hog-driving time when Eliza Blake came to the mercantile without him.

"Where's Raw Head?" the owner asked as he accepted her basket full of home remedies.

The liquid in the bottles swished in an agitated manner as Eliza Blake said, "I haven't seen him around today and I'm mighty worried. Have you seen him?"

"Nobody's seen him around today. They would've told me if they did," the mercantile owner said. "We'll keep a lookout fer you."

"That's mighty kind of you. If you see him, tell him to come home straightaway," Eliza Blake said. The mercantile owner nodded in agreement as he handed over her weekly pay.

Eliza Blake fussed to herself all the way home. It wasn't like Raw Head to disappear, especially not on shopping day. The man at the mercantile always saved the best scraps for the mean old razorback, and Raw Head never missed a visit. When the old conjuring woman got home, she mixed up a potion and poured it onto a flat plate.

"Where's that old hog gone to?" she asked the liquid. It clouded over and then a series of pictures formed. First, Eliza Blake saw the good-for-nothing hunter that lived on the next ridge sneaking around the forest, rounding up razorback hogs that didn't belong to him. One of the hogs was Raw Head. She saw him taking the hogs down to Hog-Scald Hollow, where folks from the next town were slaughtering their razorbacks. Then she saw her own hog, Raw Head, slaughtered with the rest of the pigs and hung up for gutting! The final picture in the liquid was the pile of bloody bones that had once been her hog, and his scraped-clean head lying with the other hogs' heads in a pile.

Eliza Blake was infuriated. It was murder to her, plain and simple. Everyone in three counties knew that Raw Head was her friend, and that lazy, hog-stealing, good-for-nothing hunter on the ridge was going to pay for slaughtering him.

Now Eliza Blake tried to practice white magic most of the time, but she knew the dark secrets, too. She pulled out an old, secret book her granny had given her and turned to the very last page. She lit several candles and put them around the plate containing the liquid picture of Raw Head and his bloody bones. Then she began to chant: "Raw Head and Bloody Bones. Raw Head and Bloody Bones."

The light from the windows disappeared as if the sun had been snuffed out like a candle. Dark clouds billowed into the clearing where Eliza Blake' cabin stood, and the howl of dark spirits could be heard in the wind that pummeled the treetops. "Raw Head and Bloody Bones. Raw Head and Bloody Bones."

Eliza Blake continued the chant until a bolt of silver lightning left the plate and streaked out through the window, heading in the direction of Hog-Scald Hollow.

When the silver light struck Raw Head's severed head, which was piled on the hunter's wagon with the other hog heads, it tumbled to the ground and rolled until it was touching the bloody bones that had once inhabited its body. As the hunter's wagon rumbled away toward the ridge where he lived, the enchanted Raw Head called out: "Bloody bones, get up and dance!"

Immediately, the bloody bones reassembled themselves into the skeleton of a razorback hog walking upright, as Raw Head had often done when he was alone with Eliza Blake. The head hopped on top of his skeleton, and Raw Head went searching through the woods for weapons to use against the hunter. He borrowed the sharp teeth of a dying panther, the claws of a long-dead bear, and the tail from a rotting raccoon and put them over his skinned head and bloody bones.

Then Raw Head headed up the track toward the ridge, looking for the hunter who had slaughtered him. Raw Head slipped passed the thief on the road and slid into the barn where the hunter kept his horse and wagon. He climbed up into the loft and waited for the hunter to arrive.

It was dusk when the hunter drove into the barn and unhitched his horse. The horse snorted in fear, sensing the presence of Raw Head in the loft. Wondering what was disturbing his usually calm horse, the hunter looked around and saw a large pair of eyes staring down at him from the darkness above.

The hunter frowned, thinking it was one of the local kids fooling around in his barn.

"Land o' goshen, what have you got those big eyes fer?" he snapped, thinking the kids were trying to scare him with some crazy mask.

"To see your grave," Raw Head mumbled very softly. The hunter snorted irritably and put his horse into the stall.

"Very funny. Ha, ha," The hunter said. When he came out of the stall, he saw Raw Head had crept forward a bit further.

Now his luminous yellow eyes and his bear claws could clearly be seen.

"Land o' goshen, what have you got those big claws fer?" he snapped. "You look ridiculous."

"To dig your grave," Raw Head intoned softly, his voice a deep rumble that raised the hairs on the back of the hunter's neck. He stirred uneasily, not sure how the crazy kid in his loft could have made such a scary sound—if it really was a crazy kid.

Feeling a little spooked, he hurried to the door and let himself out of the barn. Raw Head slipped off the loft and climbed down the side of the barn behind him. With nary a rustle, Raw Head raced through the trees and up the path to a large, moonlit rock. He hid in the shadow of the stone so that the only things showing were his gleaming yellow eyes, his bear claws, and his raccoon tail.

When the hunter came level with the rock on the side of the path, he gave a startled yelp. Staring at Raw Head, he gasped: "You nearly knocked the heart right out of me, you crazy kid! Land o' goshen, what have you got that crazy tail fer?"

"To sweep your grave," Raw Head boomed, his enchanted voice echoing through the woods, getting louder and louder with each echo.

At this point, the hunter took to his heels and ran for his cabin. He raced past the old well-house, past the wood pile, over the rotting fence, and into his yard. But Raw Head was faster. When the hunter reached his porch, Raw Head leapt from the shadows and loomed above him. The hunter stared in terror up at Raw Head's gleaming yellow eyes, his bloody bone skeleton with its long bear claws, sweeping raccoon's tail, and his razor-sharp panther teeth.

"Land o' goshen, what have you got those big teeth fer?" he gasped desperately, stumbling backward from the terrible figure before him.

"To eat you up, like you wanted to eat me!" Raw Head roared, descending upon the good-for-nothing hunter. The murdering thief gave one long scream in the moonlight. Then there was nothing but silence, broken by the sound of crunching.

Nothing more was ever seen or heard of the lazy hunter who lived on the ridge. His horse also disappeared that night. But sometimes folks would see Raw Head roaming through the forest in the company of his friend Eliza Blake. And once a month, on the night of the full moon, Raw Head would ride the hunter's horse through town, wearing the old man's blue overalls over his bloody bones with a hole cut out for his raccoon tail. In his bloody, bear-clawed hands, he carried his raw, razorback hog's head, lifting it high against the full moon for everyone to see.

39

The Bell Witch

Great Aunt Esther was working in the vegetable garden when I strolled through the front gate. She was a spry lady in her eighties, with a shock of white hair, snapping black eyes, and the vigor of a much younger woman. She waved a hand toward me.

"Jenny-girl! You're just in time to help me with these weeds," she called.

I grinned, picked up a trowel, and joined her in the garden.

"Shouldn't you be sitting in a rocking chair knitting or something?" I asked her.

"Shouldn't you be packing to return to that fancy school of yours?" she retorted.

"I don't leave for another week," I replied, carefully sitting down among the tomato plants. Great Aunt Esther would never forgive me if I squashed something. "Dad was saying this morning that you might be able to tell me something about the Bell Witch."

Great Aunt Esther sat back on her heels and peered at me from under the brim of her large straw hat.

"Lord, child. Whatever brought that to your mind?"

THE BELL WITCH

"Some of my friends were talking about the Bell Witch, and I thought it was interesting. You grew up near Adams, didn't you?"

"I surely did," Great Aunt Esther drawled. "And I heard more stories about the Bell Witch than I can count, each one wilder than the one before. It seems like everyone within fifty miles of Adams had at least one Bell Witch story to tell in those days."

"Did you ever meet the Bell Witch?" I asked.

"Lord, child, how old do you think I am?" Great Aunt Esther asked, quite offended by my question. "My great-granddaddy, he was the one who knew the Bell children. He and John Bell Jr. were in the Tennessee Militia together. They fought under Old Hickory in the Battle of New Orleans."

"Who is Old Hickory?" I asked.

Great Aunt Esther shook her head in despair. "Don't they teach you children anything in those fancy schools? Old Hickory was the nickname of General Andrew Jackson. You have heard of Andrew Jackson?"

"Yes, I've heard of Andrew Jackson," I snapped, embarrassed by my show of ignorance. "He was the seventh president."

"Well, at least you've learned something at that fancy boarding school of yours," Great Aunt Esther said. "When I was very small, I remember my great-granddaddy telling me about the time Old Hickory met the Bell Witch."

"Can you tell me the story?" I asked eagerly. Great Aunt Esther considered my question with a sour look on her face. She was a stickler for polite manners. I quickly amended the question. "Would you please tell me the story, Aunt Esther?"

Great Aunt Esther smiled approvingly. "I would be delighted to tell you the story, Jenny-girl. Why don't we go sit on the porch and I will get us some lemonade."

We went up to the house, washed off the dirt from our gardening, and settled into wicker chairs on the front porch with ice-cold glasses of pink lemonade. Great Aunt Esther made the best lemonade in the county.

"Now I warn you, Jenny-girl," Great Aunt Esther said, "there are probably a hundred different versions of the Bell Witch story floating around the county at any given time. All I can tell you about the Bell Witch is the story as it was told to me by my great-granddaddy. If you want 'truth' and 'facts,' you would do better to read one of the books that have been written about the Bell Witch."

"I would like to hear your story, Aunt Esther," I said promptly, bouncing a bit in my chair from pure excitement. Great Aunt Esther gave me a look that told me she did not consider my behavior up to the standards of a Southern lady. I sat still.

"The Bell family," Great Aunt Esther began, "moved to Robertson County from North Carolina sometime around 1804. They were a God-fearing family who were leading members of the community. The spirit that plagued the Bell family first made its presence known in 1817. According to my great-granddaddy, the spirit commenced its activities by rapping on the walls of the house. Shortly thereafter, it began pulling the quilts off the children's beds, tugging on their hair, and slapping and pinching them until red marks appeared on their faces and bodies. It would steal sugar right out of the bowl, spill the milk, and taunt the Bell family by laughing and cursing at them. Really, it was quite a rude spirit!" Great Aunt Esther paused to give her personal opinion. She took a dainty sip of lemonade and continued her story.

"Naturally, all this hullabaloo caused great excitement throughout the community. People would come from miles around to meet this spirit, which would gossip with them and curse at them and play tricks on them. According to my great-granddaddy, John Bell and his family would feed and entertain all these guests at their own expense—not an easy task. The house would get so full that people were forced to camp outside.

"When Old Hickory heard about the Bell Witch, he decided to pay a visit to the Bell home. The general brought a party up with him from Nashville. They filled a wagon with provisions and tents for camping out, to avoid discomfiting the Bell family.

"General Jackson and his party approached the plantation, laughing and talking about the witch and all its pranks. The men were on horseback, following the wagon with their supplies. They were boasting of how they would best the Bell Witch, when suddenly the wagon stopped short. Tug and pull as they might, the horses could not move the wagon an inch, even though they were on flat ground with no trace of mud. The driver shouted and snapped the whip, but the horses could not shift the wagon. General Jackson asked all the horsemen to dismount, and together they pushed against the wagon, to no avail. The wagon would not budge.

"Old Hickory had the men examine the wheels one by one—taking them off, checking the axles, and then reattaching them. There was nothing wrong with the wheels. They tried to move the wagon again, whipping up the horses, shouting, and pushing. But still the wagon would not budge. The men were completely flummoxed. What was going on? Then the general shouted, 'Boys, it's the witch!'

"An eerie voice answered Old Hickory from the shrubbery: 'All right, General. Let the wagon move on. I will see you again tonight.'

"The men looked around in astonishment, for they had seen no one nearby. At once, the horses started moving without any prompting from the coachman, and the wagon rumbled along the road as if it had never been stuck at all.

"Old Hickory and his men were sobered by their strange experience. Suddenly the idea of camping out was not very appealing, even though one of their men was supposed to be a professional witch tamer.

"When the general's party reached the house, John Bell and his wife extended every courtesy to their distinguished guest and his friends, offering them food, drink, entertainment, and quarters for the night. But Old Hickory had only one entertainment in mind. He had come for witch hunting, and nothing else would do. After dining with the Bells, the whole party sat waiting for the spirit to put in an appearance. To while away the time, they listened to the boasts of the witch tamer, who had a gun with a silver bullet that he meant for the spirit. The men were secretly amused by the man's vanity, yet they found his presence oddly comforting after their strange experience with the wagon. Here was someone who could handle the spirit.

"The hour grew late. Old Hickory was restless and the men were getting drowsy. The witch tamer began taunting the spirit and playing with his gun. Suddenly, there was the sound of footsteps crossing the floor. Everyone snapped to attention. Then the same eerie voice they had heard on the road exclaimed, 'I am here. Now shoot me!'

"The witch tamer aimed his gun at the place where they had heard the voice. He pulled the trigger, but the gun didn't fire. The spirit began to taunt him as the witch tamer tried to shoot the gun again. Then the spirit said, 'Now it's my turn.'

"Everyone heard the sounds of the witch tamer being slapped silly as he shouted, 'Lordy, Lordy!' and 'My nose!' and 'The devil's got me!' He began to dance about the parlor, screaming that the spirit was pricking him with pins and beating him. Then the door swung open of its own accord and the witch tamer raced outside, still shouting 'Lordy, Lordy!' as he ran down the lane. Everyone followed him outside, expecting him to drop dead, but aside from an occasional jump, twist, or shout, the witch tamer seemed likely to live. They watched him as he ran out of sight, while Old Hickory laughed until his sides were sore.

"They were all startled when they heard the spirit's voice among them again. It was laughing at its triumph over the witch tamer and claimed that there was another fraud in the group that it would expose the next night. The men were pretty shaken up when they heard the spirit's words. It was one thing to laugh at a fake witch tamer who got his comeuppance. It was quite another thing to realize one of them might be the next target. Old Hickory was all set to stay a full week with the Bells, but his men were not so enthusiastic.

"My great-granddaddy didn't know exactly what happened that night to change Old Hickory's mind. Maybe the spirit played some pranks on him, maybe the justifiable fear of his men persuaded him. Whatever the case, General Andrew Jackson was up and away the next morning. By dark, Old Hickory's party had already reached Springfield and they went on to Nashville the next day. Much later, Old Hickory was heard to remark, 'I'd rather fight the entire British Army than deal with the Bell Witch.' "

Great Aunt Esther took a sip of her lemonade and shook her head. "I don't blame the general one bit for leaving so quickly. I would have done the same thing."

"What happened to the Bell Witch, Aunt Esther?" I asked.

"Oh, most of the stories agree that the Bell Witch got worse and worse, tormenting Betsy Bell something awful and finally poisoning John Bell so that he died. They say the spirit laughed and sang in triumph at John's funeral. The spirit stayed for several months following the death of John Bell, putting pressure on Betsy to break her engagement with a man named Gardener, which Betsy did sometime around Easter of 1821. After that, the spirit told Mrs. Bell that it was going away, but would visit again in seven years."

"Did it come back?" I asked.

"Yes, the spirit did return to visit the family seven years later, just as it promised," said Great Aunt Esther. "For about three weeks, the spirit talked with John Bell Jr., making predictions about the future and promising to return in one hundred and seven years. As far as I know, the Bell family did not receive the second promised visit. I have heard some people claim that the Bell Witch never really left the Bells' property, but still haunts the land to this day. I myself have not gone there to find out if this is true."

Great Aunt Esther finished her lemonade and peered at me from under the rim of her straw hat. "Well, Jenny-girl, that's enough about evil spirits for one day. I am going back to my garden. Get along with you now, and pack your bags. School starts next week."

"Yes, ma'am," I said meekly, taking my glass back to the kitchen before I started for home. I paused at the gate.

"Aunt Esther," I called. Great Aunt Esther straightened up from among the tomato plants with a questioning frown. "Thank you for telling me your story," I said.

Great Aunt Esther smiled. "You're welcome, Jenny-girl. Tell your mama that I have fresh tomatoes. If she would care to stop by for a visit, I will offer her some."

"I'll tell her," I said. I pulled the gate shut behind me and headed for home.

40

Rupp

Pa's face was grim when he came into dinner that night.

"Someone's been messing with our cattle, Maude," he said to Mama. She looked up from the stove, her face flushed pink from the heat and little tendrils of curls hanging down into her eyes. She brushed them away impatiently.

"What do you mean?" she asked, catching up the kettle with a potholder and bringing it over to the table to pour into the teapot.

"Two of our cattle our down. And that's not the worst of it." He glanced at me as he spoke, and I straightened up indignantly. I was thirteen years old, practically a woman grown. If there was trouble coming our way, I was old enough to handle it, and I said so to Pa. His face softened a fraction, and he tousled my hair. Then he told us what he'd found.

Two of our cows had been dismembered in a back field. The head and hindquarters were all that remained of the cattle, and when Pa investigated the grisly remains, he found that they'd been drained of every drop of blood.

Mama went pale when she heard this. There was a story told in her family about a great aunt who'd died in mysterious

RUPP

circumstances over in Europe a long time ago. She too had been drained of blood, and her family thought she'd been killed by a vampire who'd been stalking young women in their town for several years.

We were all thinking about the story, but none of us said the word aloud. We didn't want to jinx ourselves, although I couldn't think of anything else that would drain all the blood out of a creature. I shuddered, and Pa patted my shoulder reassuringly.

"I'm sure there's a logical explanation for it," he said unconvincingly. "Maybe a bear got them."

"A bear that drinks blood?" There, I'd said it. Mama winced and turned away.

"Just you keep your window closed at night, Katie," Pa said, and that was that—end of conversation, end of mystery.

But it wasn't the end of the story. No, we'd only just begun.

Three days later our neighbor lost a cow under the same mysterious circumstances. Then a family on the other side of the ridge. And then a farmer on the far side of town. There were lots of foreigners around these days, men who had come from Europe to work in the mines. And they'd heard of vampires, just like we had, though I doubted any of them had lost family to one.

A few days later a number of prominent townsmen just "happened" to drop into the tavern after supper to discuss the matter. Most had lived in these parts all their lives, but there were a few newcomers too. All of them seemed above suspicion, though Mama made Pa carry garlic and a silver cross, just in case.

During the meeting, the names of several men were bandied about, all of them newcomers and all of them miners. Everyone seemed to think it was one of them behind the cattle killings. After all, the men went down into the mines before daylight and came up after dark—a perfect setup for a vampire. No one came to any conclusion that night, but when Pa got home, he warned Mama and me to stay away from the mine, just in case.

My best friend Joshua, who lived next door, came over after chores the next afternoon to discuss the mysterious cattle killings. "I have an idea about that," he said importantly, swinging himself up onto the paddock fence and leaning his back against the post. "There's that weird fellow living on the other side of the ridge. Rupp he calls himself. He's a newcomer and he works in the mines. And no cattle went missing before he arrived."

I considered this. Rupp was a sort of neighbor of ours. We had to pass the turnoff to his remote cabin on our way to town. I'd only seen him once or twice, but each time something about him had frightened me. He was tall, thin, and pale, with blood-red lips and narrow dark eyes. It was the look in those eyes that made me want to run away whenever I saw him. They had a hungry look that made my skin crawl. And the two times I'd seen him had both been at night. I'd never seen him during the day.

"Of course he's in the mine during the day," I said, continuing my thought out loud. Josh must have been following the expressions on my face, for he responded to my comment as if I'd spoke my previous thoughts aloud.

"He says he's in the mines during the day," he said. "We have no proof that he's really there."

"But don't they have to sleep in their coffins or something like that?" I asked, trying to remember the details about my great-aunt's supposed killer. "Rudd lives in a one-room cabin. A coffin would be pretty obvious."

"Not if it's up in the loft. I'm going to check," Josh said, slipping down off the fence post.

"I'm coming too," I said. Josh froze in his tracks and then turned, a fierce, protective look on his face.

"You are going to stay right here with your pa and mama," he said. "I don't want you anywhere near Rupp. Do you hear me?"

I was startled and flushed a little at the look on his face. A few times that spring, I'd wondered if Josh thought of me as more than a friend. Now I was certain.

"Promise me, Kate," he said sternly.

I promised.

"I'll take Fred along. Safety in numbers," he said. Fred was the neighbor on the other side of Josh. He was a big, strong lad a few years older than Josh and me. I nodded approvingly. They should be safe. I hoped.

We were sitting down to dinner when Josh and Fred came bursting into the kitchen.

"Rupp," Josh gasped, his eyes going straight to my father. "Rupp."

Fred grabbed my father by the arm, and the boys dragged him outside into the yard. Mama and I rushed to the window to watch and listen. The three of them stood by the paddock fence. We could hear their voices, but a storm was blowing up, and the wind whipped their words away before we could make them out. We saw Pa's face go grim, and then he left with the boys, heading toward town.

Mama told me to close all the windows and lock the doors. She got out the garlic and some of the holy amulets passed down in her family and draped them over us. Then we sat down in front of the fireplace and waited for Pa to come home.

It was late when we heard someone fumbling at the front door. We glanced at each other, bodies tensed. Then we heard a key in the lock and knew it was Pa. He came wearily in and saw our worried faces at once in the shadowy firelight.

"The boys looked through the cabin window and saw Rupp gnawing on a raw calf leg," he said without preamble. "We spoke to the sheriff about it, but he said it isn't against the law to eat raw meat. Folks in the tavern were pretty agitated by the sheriff's attitude, but his hands are tied, since there's no actual proof that the cow's leg came from one of the mutilated animals. No proof," he repeated, as if trying to convince himself. But the look on his face told us he was convinced that Rupp was behind the dead cattle.

Rumors buzzed around town for several days after Josh and Fred's visit to Rupp's cabin, but as the weeks passed without another dead cow, things settled down. Then the town drunk went missing. Of course he went missing twice a month, regular, right after he got a paycheck. But this was different. He was still a week shy of getting paid, and he hadn't shown up for several days. Finally the sheriff went looking for him and found his body in the valley a quarter mile below Rupp's cabin. He was drained of blood and missing an arm and a leg.

Unfortunately, Rupp's was not the only home near the valley where the murdered man was found. The sheriff had to question everyone who lived nearby, including us. Everyone denied knowledge of the murder, including Rupp, who didn't show up at his cabin until well after dark on the day the body was found. He spoke to the sheriff at length in the small clearing outside his cabin but did not invite him inside, and the sheriff couldn't force the issue without a search warrant, which he didn't have.

The sheriff stopped by our house after his interview with Rupp to talk to Pa, who was a good friend of his. The two men decided the sheriff should apply to the judge for a search warrant for Rupp's place, if only to dispel the rumors surrounding the man. It was at least a two-day trip and could take even longer if the judge wasn't home.

The sheriff headed out to the county courthouse the next morning, so he didn't hear about the traveling salesman who hadn't shown up to breakfast at the inn. The innkeeper's wife was alarmed when she went to make up his room and found the bed hadn't been slept in. The man's horse was still in the inn stable. But he was missing.

We heard all about it at school that day. Everyone discussed it over lunch and decided that the vampire must have gotten the salesman either right before or right after he talked to the sheriff. All the girls, even me, shuddered at the thought, and Josh boldly took my hand to comfort me. He held my hand all through lunch and smiled shyly at me as we parted at the school door to go to our separate desks.

I had to run a few errands in town for Mama after school, and I lingered too long in the grocery, looking longingly through the new book of dress patterns that had just arrived. It was dusk when I set off on the road home, my basket clenched at my side. The road was long and winding and already nearly dark in the shadow of the tall trees on either side. I kept remembering the story of the dismembered drunk and the missing salesman as I walked alone down the road. Normally the nighttime woods were my friend. But not now. Not since Rupp came.

I shuddered at the thought, remembering that I had to pass the lane leading toward Rupp's cabin. I quickened my pace, wanting to be well away from the spot before true darkness fell. I wished that I had asked Josh to come on my errands with me. But I knew he had chores to do, so I hadn't.

The wind whistled mournfully through the tops of the trees as I hastened down the darkening road. The smallest sounds made me jump: the rustle of small creatures in the underbrush, the hoot of a newly awakened owl, the raucous squawking of a crow. I hugged the basket close to me, walking as fast as I could. I saw Rupp's lane ahead and sped up until I was almost running. My eyes kept straying toward the sinister, overgrown lane—more of a deer trail than a proper road. And that's how I spotted the man's shoe sticking out of the underbrush a few yards down the lane.

I stopped suddenly, my whole body prickling with terror. Oh, no, I thought. Please don't let it be the salesman. I wanted to run for home, but I couldn't pass by without looking. What if it had been Pa who'd gone missing, or Josh? I'd have wanted to know.

I crept cautiously down the lane, the basket held in front of me like a shield. I parted the bush above the shoe, and a wave of nausea filled me as I spied the deathly white face and dismembered body of a man in a travel suit. I gasped, my whole body shaking in reaction to the sight. And then I froze as behind me a voice hissed, "Hello, little girl. What brings you here on this lovely night?"

It was Rupp.

I whirled with a shriek and pressed my back into the bush that held the salesman's body. "H . . . hello, Mr. Rupp," I whispered, holding the basket up between us. "I thought I saw something in the bushes, but it was j . . . just a trick of the light," I lied desperately.

The vampire's dark eyes glowed with a reddish glint in the dim twilight. His pale face was almost ruddy with the new blood he'd taken from his victim. It was obvious that he didn't believe my story. It was also obvious that I was not going to make it out of this situation alive. He smiled at me in the gloaming, and I saw two incisors slowly lengthen into sharp points as he raised his hands toward my throat.

And then another voice came from the main road: "Kate! Katie! Are you there?"

It was Josh, coming to look for me. His words were echoed immediately by a deeper man's voice. Pa.

"Here!" I screamed. "Here!"

Quick as a flash, Rupp disappeared into the woods beside me. So light on his feet was the vampire that I did not hear a rustle or a twig crack.

Pa and Josh came running into the lane, and I fell into their arms, babbling desperately about Rupp and the dead salesman in the bushes behind me. Pa took one look into the shrubbery and sent me home with Josh. I clung to my best friend, weeping and explaining how Rupp had appeared from nowhere and how he had reached for my throat. When I mentioned Rupp's elongated incisors, my voice went all to pieces and Josh looked rather murderous himself. He explained that they'd grown worried when I wasn't home by dusk and had come to look for me, knowing I'd have to pass Rupp's lane on my way home.

"Thank God we did," he added fervently, hugging me close to him.

Josh made sure I was safe in my mother's arms before he returned to town with Pa to see what the men meant to do about Rupp. Mama and I were preparing for bed when we heard shouts coming from the lane down the road. Rushing to an upper window, we saw through the trees the flickering light of torches heading toward Rupp's place. Not long after, we saw a massive fire reaching up and up to the sky and knew the vampire's cabin was burning.

Pa came in around midnight, and we both rushed downstairs to meet him.

"He's gone," Pa said, sinking wearily into a kitchen chair. "We searched everywhere, but he knew we'd be after him after he threatened Kate, and he bolted. The cabin was full of blood and gore and dismembered body parts—some of them human."

Pa's face went a bit green at the memory, and for a moment I was afraid he'd lose his dinner. But he recovered after a moment and went on: "Search parties scoured the woods around the cabin, but we found nothing. So, we torched the cabin to discourage him from coming back. We'll start the search again at first light, but my guess is he's gone."

And Pa was right. The posse combed the woods for several days in a row, while folks in town and the outlying farms held their breath in fear. But there was no sign of Rupp. By the time the sheriff returned to town with his now-useless search warrant, everyone agreed that the vampire calling himself Rupp had fled the county.

Mama made me carry garlic and holy amulets on me whenever I went outside that autumn and winter. But by the time spring rolled around, even she was convinced that the vampire was gone. She and Pa strictly forbade me to go near the burned-out cabin in the woods. Not that they needed to. I still had nightmares about that moment I'd found the dismembered body of the traveling salesman in the bushes and heard Rupp's voice behind me. I probably always would.

Some folks in town say the men overreacted that night. They say Rupp was a sadistic killer, but no vampire. But Josh and I know better. He bought me a silver cross for my last birthday and had it specially blessed by a priest. When he gave it to me, he made me promise that I would wear it around my neck all the days of my life and never take it off. That's a vow I intend to keep!

41

The Floating Coffin

The soldier shifted uneasily in the saddle as he waved goodbye to his sweetheart. She was standing on the front porch. The lantern lit her lovely face with a soft glow that made her luminous dark eyes shine. His heart swelled at the sight. He sent her a sizzling smile that made the lovely color rise in her cheeks. Then he turned his horse jauntily and trotted down the darkened twist of road that led through the forest to his home in the next town.

As soon as he rounded the first corner, out of sight of his love, the soldier slowed his horse to a walk and took an apprehensive breath. Just a mile from his sweetheart's farm was the local cemetery, and he must ride past it to get to his home. Normally not a fearful man—or an imaginative one—the soldier nonetheless dreaded riding past the cemetery during the day and it absolutely terrified him at night.

This makes no sense, he scolded himself for the thousandth time as he picked up a slow trot through the dim starlight. He'd past hundreds of graveyards all over the South during the Civil War and none had bothered him before.

THE FLOATING COFFIN

Of course, none of those cemeteries were in West Virginia, his conscious murmured. None were near the scene of the incident.

The soldier shied away from the thought. There was only one blot on his spotless career. One terrible, insane moment. It had been swept under the carpet as just one more of the many insane, terrible moments that occurred during that terrible war.

The crime happened during the Jones-Imboden raid, where the soldier fought side-by-side with his baby brother, whom he'd sworn to protect on the deathbed of their beloved mother. One moment the brothers were fighting together and the next moment the younger brother was twenty yards away. As the soldier fought his way toward his brother, he saw a Confederate shoot his baby brother through the head. The Confederate grinned viciously as his brother fell to the ground at his feet. The soldier's whole world went red. He screamed with rage and charged the man, only to be swept aside by a column of fighting boys in blue. By the time the rush dissipated, the Confederate was gone. But the man's visage was forever burned into the soldier's mind. He swore, as he tenderly picked up the body, that he would hunt down the man and kill him for the sake of his dead brother.

The soldier was as good as his word. Each night he'd slip out of his tent and seek out nearby Confederate camps, searching for his enemy. But nary a scrap or hair did he see. By the final day of the campaign, the soldier resigned himself to failure.

He was among the officers charged to guard the wounded and prisoners as the Union army marched away. Diligently, the soldier rode down the line, checking the status of the injured and watching over the enemy prisoners. As he approached the last wagon, the soldier saw a familiar figure sitting in the back with the other prisoners. The world turned red before his eyes and his vision narrowed until all he saw was the face of his enemy. The soldier didn't hesitate. He rode up to the wagon, pointed his pistol at the bound man's head and pulled the trigger. Then he turned his horse and rode to the front of the line without a backward glance. None of the Union soldiers on duty that day reported the murder. What was one more Confederate death to them?

The next day the soldier asked for a transfer and he fought the rest of the Civil war on the Western front. When the war ended, the soldier returned to his home in West Virginia and bought a farm in the county where he grew up. He'd prospered there and had found himself a lovely sweetheart. Which was how he came to be riding down this blasted road at night, right past a haunted cemetery.

A sudden rustle of wind in the trees shook the soldier out of his grim memories. It sounded like the dry warning of a rattlesnake. The soldier shuddered, suddenly cold, and his fingers tightened on the reins until his horse tossed its head uncomfortably.

He hated the cemetery passionately. Whenever he rode beside the iron fence, the soldier's eye was drawn to an unadorned burial mound in the far corner. Such mounds, he knew, contained the bodies of Confederate soldiers; buried near the place they fell in battle. Every time the soldier saw this particular grave, chills ran down his spine and he relived the moment when he put a pistol to a helpless man's head and pulled the trigger. The look of terror in the man's eyes still froze his blood.

Starlight gleamed on the ironwork of the cemetery fence as the soldier's horse drew level with it; but the graves beyond were dark and full of menacing shadows. A chill wind, whispering of murder and death, tried to blow the soldier from his horse as he rode down the empty road. Dread filled his gut and cold sweat dripped down his neck, but he refused to look toward the shadowed mound at the back of the cemetery. Enough was enough. He was not a coward. He'd lived through a terrible war and won a new life for himself. Let the past go.

Suddenly, there came a sharp explosion like a canon going off and a brilliant light blazed from the back of the cemetery. The soldier's horse screamed and reared in terror, and the soldier fought desperately for his balance. The horse gave a mad twist that toppled soldier to the road and it galloped away at top speed. The soldier lay panting; stunned by his fall. His heart was pounding with terror and he fought for each breath. What was that explosion? And how could there possibly be so much light in the middle of the night?

The unnatural light drew closer. The soldier's skin crawled. He wanted to run away. But where could he go without his horse? Better to face whatever it was like a man. He groped for his pistol with trembling hands, cursed when he realized he wasn't carrying it, and then leapt to his feet with a shout, hoping to scare whatever it was away with the sudden noise.

Then he froze in shock; unable to move or think. An open coffin floated a few feet from the place where he lay. Standing on top of it was a rotting corpse. Just enough of the face was left for the soldier to identify the reddish beard and rotting blue eyes of the Confederate prisoner he'd murdered during the War. The Confederate's legs were still bound with a filthy white cloth, and there was a gaping wound in the center of the forehead where the bullet had struck.

"Nooooo!" The soldier screamed, flinching away from the rotting phantom. The coffin floated closer, and the Confederate reached out toward the soldier with bony, skin-shredded fingers.

The smell of death and decay overwhelmed the soldier, breaking through his paralysis. He screamed and fled down the dark road, the coffin floating just behind him. It gained speed and suddenly he felt it bump the back of his legs, tripping him. The soldier stumbled and fell to the ground. Decaying hands lifted the soldier and turned him to face his enemy. The Confederate grinned at him through broken black teeth. The soldier could see maggots eating the flesh of its cheek. He vomited at the sight; the acrid smell mixing horribly with the smells of dust and rot pouring from his enemy. As the soldier hung helplessly in the phantom's grip, the Confederate reached through the bullet hole in its rotting skull and plucked out the bullet lodged in its dead brain. With a vicious smile, the Confederate placed the bullet against the soldier's forehead. The bullet became red-hot, burning the soldier's flesh. He screamed in anguish as the Confederate pushed the bullet through the bone and into the soldier's brain.

When the soldier did not return to his farm, the neighbors set out to look for him. As they past the cemetery on the way to inquire at his sweetheart's home, the neighbors saw that a grave mound at the back had been disturbed. Dirt was scattered everywhere, as if the coffin had been violently thrust from the earth by some supernatural force. The splintered box lay askew a few yards from the mound, its lid broken in half. Inside the coffin lay the body of the soldier, his dead face twisted in horror and a bullet hole drilled through his skull. The corpse of the coffin's former occupant had vanished.

42

Buried Alive

It was a cold autumn. I wasn't surprised when Mama, who had a weak constitution, caught a chill. She became quite ill, and nothing the doctor did seemed to help. After several nights of restlessness and high fever, she suddenly grew cold and stopped breathing. I was stricken when I brought her lunch upstairs and found that she was gone.

We were all heartbroken; Papa most of all. It was a cold, windy day in November when family, friends, and servants gathered in the garden to lay poor Mama to rest. I wept bitterly and could not be comforted. On the other side of the open grave the family butler hovered, glaring bitterly at Papa. My father's sturdy frame shook with grief as the minister spoke the eulogy. He didn't notice the butler's anger, but I did. The butler wasn't upset about Mama's death. No, he was angry over some slight one of the family members had given him that morning. To me, it was a trifling thing compared with the tragic death of our mother, but he could not forget it.

Later I heard the butler in the kitchen, complaining to the cook about all the valuable jewelry that had been buried with

BURIED ALIVE

my mother. "First they insult me, and then they waste all that money on a dead woman," he said loudly.

"Hush," the cook said, nervously glancing about. "The Family will not tolerate such talk."

"The Family!" the butler said, his face turning beat red. "I'll tell you what I think of the Family." He started swearing then, using words I'd never heard before and didn't care to know the meaning of. I clapped my hands over my ears and hurried away, shocked at such behavior.

As my maid prepared me for bed that night, I saw a light flashing in the garden. Curious, I glanced outside and saw the butler stalking down the garden toward the family graveyard carrying a lantern. The sight made me uneasy. He must be on an errand for the Papa, I thought. But my skin prickled as I remembered his words in the kitchen.

Instead of going to bed, I made my way downstairs and mentioned what I'd seen to one of the footmen and to the cook, who was washing up the last of the dishes. "I'm sure he's doing something for your Papa," Cook said reassuringly. "He was just talking nonsense before to relieve his feelings. I wouldn't worry about it, my dear."

Somewhat reassured, I hurried upstairs. As I silently passed Papa's study, I caught a glimpse of him through the open door. He was standing in front of a roaring fire, his face sad. I knocked on the doorframe. When Papa looked up, I hurried in to give him a comforting hug. Outside, the wind picked up and I caught a glimpse of snowflakes piling up against the window. I shivered, imagining my poor cold mother buried under the snow. Tears poured down my cheeks and I buried my face against Papa's shoulder as I wept.

After leaving the study, I paused on the landing and glanced out the window to see if I could spot the butler going about his errand for Papa. I still felt terribly uneasy, in spite of Cook's words. I glimpsed a faint light glowing in the family graveyard and thought for a moment that I heard a shout of alarm. But it may have only been the wind gusting against the house as the snow began falling in earnest.

I went to bed but couldn't sleep. After tossing and turning for nearly an hour, I rose, dressed, and went down to the kitchen for a drink of water. Cook was still there, sitting in front of the fire with her cup. She smiled when she saw me, a sympathetic smile. She knew how close I'd been to my mother. Her compassionate look brought tears again, and she held me close and let me weep until the rush of pain had passed. Then she made me drink a hot cup of tea.

As I swallowed my tea, I heard someone knock at the kitchen door. Cook looked surprised.

"Who could that be at this time of night?" she muttered. She hustled across the room and opened the door. Then she screamed so loud that she woke the whole house. I heard thumps upstairs as people leapt out of their beds, and voices exclaimed in surprise. I ran toward Cook to see what was wrong. And saw my mother kneeling in the snow by the kitchen door, cradling a bleeding hand.

"It's a ghost! The Missus has returned as a ghost," Cook wailed.

I reeled backward in horror at the sight. Why had mother returned as a ghost?

A crowd of servants had descended upon the kitchen, summoned by Cook's scream. At the sight of my mother's ghost, they too screamed, gasping and wringing their hands.

I stood frozen in my bathrobe and slippers, unable to move, my eyes taking in the grisly spectacle. Mama knelt on the stoop, pale as a ghost. Behind her, I could see a trail of blood leading back toward the graveyard. That didn't make sense. Do corpses bleed, I wondered. I didn't think they did. That's when I realized the truth. "Oh, dear God," I cried. "We buried her alive!"

I flung myself toward my kneeling mother and the servants pulled me back, afraid of what the phantom might do to me.

Papa arrived, thrusting his way through the masses. He gasped when he saw Mama on the stoop.

"Martha," he shouted, breaking the spell of horror that had overtaken all of us. Papa leapt into the snow and pulled Mother's body inside. "She's breathing," he cried a moment later. "She's alive! Quickly someone summon the doctor. And get blankets to warm her. Build up the fire."

A living woman was a far cry from a ghostly haunting. Papa was overwhelmed by servants rushing about trying to make themselves useful.

"Dear God, what happened to her hand?" Papa asked, trying to mop up the blood with his handkerchief.

I hung back, still unnerved by the sight of my living mother after I'd seen her buried earlier in the day. There was a bloody stump where one of her fingers had been cut off. That finger had borne an expensive ruby ring when she was buried. I noticed that all the jewelry had been stripped from her body. I shivered suddenly, all the little clues slowly coming together in my shocked mind.

The kitchen door was still open, and I looked out at the snowy ground and once again saw the trail of blood, rapidly being covered by snowflakes.

"How did Mama get out of the coffin?" I asked suddenly. "It was buried under the ground."

Papa's head jerked up. He stared at me, mouth agape. The whole kitchen went still.

"And where's all her jewelry? She had a ruby ring on the finger that is missing."

"We'd best find out," Papa said, suddenly grim. He tenderly handed Mama to her lady's maid and stalked out the door with several footmen. I borrowed Cook's shawl and followed. I was convinced the butler was behind all this. But he'd probably already run away.

We followed the faint trail of blood in the snow. The marks indicated that Mama had walked—no, had crawled—from the graveyard to the door.

Ahead of me, I heard my father swearing and the footmen exclaiming in horror. I skidded up beside them and looked down on a six-foot hole in the ground. The coffin gaped open, but it wasn't empty. Inside lay the butler, face down. He wasn't moving. A shovel and a spilled sack full of my mother's jewelry sat at the edge of the hole. The lantern lay extinguished on its side in the new fallen snow.

"Lying, smirking thief!" My father was still shouting.

"But sir, it was probably the shock of the cut finger that woke her up," one of the footmen said cautiously. "She must have sprung up suddenly and scared the butler half to death.

Look at the marks in the snow! Here's where the Missus sprang up and out of the tomb. And these are the butler's footprints. He tried to run away, but he slipped right here and fell into the grave instead. He must have knocked himself out when he fell, otherwise he'd be long gone by now."

My father stopped in mid-sputter. The footman was right.

"Wake him up and get him out of there," Papa said finally. "We will take him to the constable, though I will probably not prosecute him as thoroughly as he deserves."

The footmen slid cautiously into the hole. Then one yelped: "He's dead! Sir, he's dead!"

They hoisted the body up, and we realized the butler had landed on his own knife when he fell into the coffin. Which seemed a fitting end.

The doctor reattached Mama's finger and made her stay in bed for a week to recover from her ordeal. She couldn't remember anything that happened between the time she fell into her coma until the time she found herself crawling through the snow toward the kitchen door with a throbbing hand. Which was probably a blessing.

We had the butler buried in the local graveyard. I didn't know whether to curse him or thank him. Papa routinely did both. But there's no doubt that if it weren't for him, Mama would not be with us today. So, on balance, I think it was worth it.

43

Boo Hag

BEAUFORT, SOUTH CAROLINA

Ever since he was a little tyke playing at his Granny's knee, George had heard about the boo hag that rode a man that was sleeping, stealing his every breath away until his life was sucked clean out of him. According to Granny, boo hags had no skin, and they gleamed all red and gory, with their veins and arteries pulsing beneath flailed muscle. To hide among humans, they stole a victim's skin and used it for as long as it held out, wearing it as one might wear clothing. Of course, they removed the skin before going riding. The hag entered a victim's home through a small crack or hole. Then it positioned itself over the sleeping victim and sucked their breath, rendering the victim helpless, and inducing a deep dream-filled sleep. Often, the hag left its victim alive since it wanted to harvest the victim's energy as long as possible. But when the victim struggled, the hag stole their skin, leaving the victim to suffer. After sucking the victim's energy all night, the hag flew off, since it had to be in its skin by dawn or be forever trapped without skin.

When George was a little boy, he'd believed every word of the story, and kept a broom next to his bedside every night, to make sure the boo hag—who was obsessed with counting—

BOO HAG

would be so captivated by all the bristles to count on the head of that broom that she'd leave him alone.

But that was when he was a small boy. These days, George was working hard at his very own smithy. He shoed all the horses for miles around and earned himself a good living. And, he had to admit, he played hard too. Not so hard that he lost all his cash, no sir. But he enjoyed drinking with his buddies at the local bar, and he'd squired more than one young lady to the local dances. George had no time to spare for the silly old legends that his Granny—God rest her soul—had believed in. There was no such thing as a boo hag. It was just a story told to frighten the kiddies into behaving themselves.

Now a new family had just moved to Beaufort, and they had a beautiful daughter with sparkling eyes and sassy ways. Nancy had all the fellows in Beaufort panting after her within a week of setting foot in the place, but she was a picky sort, and encouraged all of them equally.

George heard talk about Nancy long before he set eyes on her. His customers came into the smithy while he was hammering away at horseshoes and talked George's ear off about the new girl. George listened thoughtfully but didn't say much. It was his private opinion that the lady was spoiled by all the attention from the fellows. He didn't reckon he'd enter the ranks of men fighting over Nancy. There were plenty of girls in Beaufort that were sweet as well as pretty. He'd keep on squiring them to the local dances and let the other fellows fight over Nancy.

But that was before George saw Nancy for the first time. He was standing at the back of the church on the Sunday after Nancy's family moved to town and his heart leapt straight out of his chest when he saw the lovely girl poised in the doorway of the church. George's legs gave out on him, and he sat down hard on the pew beside him, his mouth agape. Lucky for him, everyone was swarming around Nancy, and no one saw his predicament. By the time Nancy and her folks walked to their pew, George was calmly reading his Bible. He didn't look up at Nancy as she passed, a fact that nettled the pretty girl. She snuck glances all through the service at the handsome blacksmith sitting in the last pew and wondered why he wasn't looking her way like all the other fellows were doing. She'd looked forward to adding the blacksmith to her conquests, and here he was ignoring her completely!

George figured his best chance at winning Nancy was to play hard to get, so he gave a polite nod when they were introduced after church and then turned his considerable charms on her widowed aunt. Later, he walked home with a local girl who was training at Penn School to be a midwife. Nancy turned to her widowed aunt and pouted: "What a flirt that man is! I hope the boo hag finds him and gives him a proper ride!"

Nancy's auntie gave her a penetrating look and said: "Shame on you, girl. What a thing to wish on a good, honest man, just because he isn't panting after you!"

Nancy was startled, then ashamed. "I didn't mean it," she mumbled to the air in general, just in case a boo hag was lurking among the moss-strewn oak trees.

"I should hope not," her auntie scolded her. "Now choose one of your beaus and come on home. Your Mama will have dinner on the table before you've even left the church yard!"

Nancy thought about the elusive blacksmith all the way back to her house, and for many weeks to come. George stuck to his plan, and he escorted all the other girls to the parties and church socials, leaving Nancy to her panting hordes of bachelors. Nancy was in a tizzy about the whole thing. Despite her auntie's warning, she kept on wishing that a boo hag would take the handsome blacksmith down a peg or two.

About a month later, the whole town gathered near the water's edge for a church picnic. George was paying court to a couple of pretty farmers' daughters, pushing them back and forth on a swing he'd cobbled together from a few lengths of rope and an old board. Nancy was surrounded by swains. She divided her attention between sweet-talking the bachelors into bringing her sweets from the picnic tables and glaring at George, who was telling an amusing tale to the farmers' daughters and their friends.

"I wish a boo hag would ride him right out of town," she muttered under her breath. Then she forced a smile as one of her beaus came eagerly to her, carrying two glasses of lemonade.

Lurking near the water's edge a few yards from Nancy was a boo hag, disguised as an old washerwoman. The boo hag was hungry. She had ridden a man to death down in Georgia a few weeks ago but had no luck finding another victim since then. Hearing Nancy's careless words, the boo hag eyed George thoughtfully. Here was a strapping young man, wide of shoulder and strong of arm. He would make a good feast.

The old washerwoman watched the blacksmith thoughtfully from her hiding place by the river, as he wandered through the fields, joking with the bachelors, talking piously with the minister, flirting with the girls. Nancy, dispirited by George's indifference, wandered away from her beaus and stood looking out over the river, wondering what she could do to make the handsome blacksmith like her. George, who was watching her from afar, came casually down to the water's edge, a few feet from the hidden boo hag. His heart was pounding nervously against his ribs as he approached the lovely girl, though he kept his face cool and composed.

"What's troubling you, Nancy?" he asked.

Startled, the girl whirled to face the tall, handsome man who'd caught her fancy from the moment she laid eyes on him in church.

"Why should I be troubled?" Nancy asked, her heart thundering so loud she thought George must hear it. "It's a lovely day and everyone's having a good time at the picnic."

"Everyone's having a good time, except you," George corrected her. "Why are you down here all alone?" He took her hand. And Nancy, looking up into the blacksmith's dark eyes, discovered she wasn't alone anymore. She would never be alone again.

George walked Nancy home from the church picnic that evening, and it was quite clear to the other bachelors that Nancy had completely forgotten all her other beaus. From that moment on, she was spoken for.

George was walking on air when he headed home after kissing Nancy for the first time on her front porch. He never noticed the old washerwoman trailing behind him. He felt no urge to buy blue paint as he passed the hardware shop, and he left his old broom down in the smithy when he climbed upstairs to bed.

He had only been asleep a few minutes when the washerwoman whirled and twirled in a frenzy of motion until her borrowed skin fell away, revealing the red blood vessels and flailed flesh of a boo hag. She magicked herself small enough to fit through George's keyhole and floated inside the blacksmith's bedroom to lay herself across his mouth and steal a part of every breath he took. And with each breath, she took a piece of his soul.

George's dreams were filled with visions of Nancy that night. He woke dazed and happy, though for some reason he was feeling rather more tired than usual. He put his unsteadiness down to the giddiness of love and got to work down in the smithy. But his hands were not steady on his tools, and he had more difficulty than usual calming the horses. They pulled away from him, nostrils flaring, as if there was a stench on him that they found distressing. It troubled George enough that he heated water for himself that evening and took a long bath to wash off the smell before heading out to see Nancy. They sat on the porch with her family, watching the sun set on the river and singing old songs. George's voice kept faltering. He was short of breath, and Nancy thought he looked a little pale.

All that week and the next, the boo hag visited George's rooms each night, sucking the breath and the life out of him, little by little. George had strange dreams all night. During the day, his eyes were glassy and feverish, his hands were unsteady, and he grew pale under his tan. His big body trembled as he stood, and he found his tools harder and harder to lift. Horses reared when he came near them, something they had never done before.

Nancy was alarmed by the radical change in her beau. She called the doctor to come and look at George. The doctor shook his head and prescribed a tonic to be drunk twice a day, but it didn't help George. He kept losing weight and he could hardly catch his breath. It was all he could do to keep up with the easiest of his smithing tasks. The heavy work was almost beyond him.

Nancy's old aunt was away visiting kinfolk up in Charleston when George started courting Nancy. But she returned to Beaufort at the end of the second week, right around the time George was taken so badly it looked like he'd have to give up smithing until the mysterious disease was cured. After interviewing George about his illness, the old aunt pulled Nancy aside and said: "Nancy, I want you to run to the hardware store and get some blue paint. Be quick about it. There's no time to spare."

"Blue paint? Why do you want blue paint?" Nancy asked her old aunt, wide-eyed.

"Think girl!" The aunt scolded her pretty niece. "It was you who wished a boo hag on that young man. Now he's got one, and it's killing him. Everyone knows the only way to keep a boo hag out of a house is to paint the windows and doorways with blue paint. A boo hag can't fly through a window or door that's painted blue. Be quick now, while George's still talking to your Pa."

Nancy was stricken to the bone. She remembered all the times she'd wished a boo hag would ride George because he wasn't paying attention to her. Now George was rapidly losing strength and could never catch his breath, all on account of her.

Nancy flew down the road to the hardware store and bought a can of blue paint and a brush. Then she slipped over to the smithy and painted all the doors and windows blue. As soon as she finished her task, Nancy hurried back home, slipping in the door just as supper was served. Over dinner, she caught her aunt's eye and nodded to let her know the job was done.

George went home after supper, walking stiff and weary as if he were an old man of seventy instead of a strapping young lad in his prime. Nancy watched him go with her heart in her mouth. "Please let the blue paint work," she prayed as she climbed into bed. If it didn't work, George was sure to die. The boo hag had ridden him hard for two weeks, and he could barely stand on his own.

Nancy woke a little before dawn the next morning, her heart pounding. She was sure she had missed something at George's house. She reviewed her work in her mind. She'd painted the door of the smith, and both windows, and the two big windows on the second story, front and back, and the little windows on the sides. And then she remembered. She'd forgotten the tiny window in the loft over George's bedroom. The window was always kept open a crack so the tiny owl George had rescued as a boy and kept as a pet could fly in and out of the house whenever it chose.

Nancy leapt out of bed, threw on a wrapper, and ran downstairs to wake her auntie. She was almost incoherent with fear as she told her aunt what she'd left undone. A moment later, two grim-faced women hurried down the road toward the smithy, hair a-tangle and robes flapping around their bare feet. Old auntie was clutching a keg of sea salt in her gnarled hands. "Pray God we are in time," she said.

When they reached the smithy, the aunt told Nancy to grab the old broom standing against the wall. Wielding it like a sword, the two women advanced up the steps to the upper room and banged open the door. The room was gently lit by the fire in the hearth. George was sleeping on the bed, his handsome face lit by an unnatural smile. Hovering over him was a gleaming boo hag, all flailed muscle and bone and hideously pulsing arteries. When the women burst into the room, the boo hag whirled upward with a shriek of rage. Then her eyes fixed on the besom in Nancy's hands. A boo hag cannot resist counting the straws in a broom when it sees one, and the evil creature swept down from the ceiling and seized the broom, yanking it away from Nancy and pulling the brush closer to her face.

On the bed, George woke with a start and stared in amazement at the sight of the boo hag, hovering in the center of the room and of his beloved and her auntie, clad in long white nightgowns and wrappers, confronting the pulsing red creature. He sat bolt upright with a shout of his own.

The boo hag looked up, distracted by George's sudden movement, and old auntie seized her chance. Stepping forward, she threw the entire keg of salt over the boo hag where it hovered with the broom in its gleaming red hand. The boo hag gave a howl of agony, the salt burning through her exposed muscle and bone. She sailed desperately upward, trying to brush away the salt, making for the small window which she'd entered in the loft. If she could immerse herself in the river, the effects of the salt would be mitigated, and the boo hag would survive to feast upon another victim. But at that moment, the first rays of the sun shimmered across the horizon, streaming in the little window of the loft and piercing right through the creature. The boo hag gave a shriek of agony and burst into flames. The salt on her skinless body sizzled and sparked, and then the boo hag disappeared in a puff of smoke and fiery brimstone.

Nancy gave a heartfelt cry of relief and joy. She raced across the room and flung herself into George's arms, weeping with relief. Old auntie followed at a more sedate pace to chaperone the pair and explain to the puzzled George the true cause of his ailment.

George recovered his strength rapidly once the boo hag was dead. He and Nancy were married a fortnight later in the Brick Church where they first met. Nancy faithfully promised her old auntie that she'd never wish a boo hag on another person, as long as she lived. And George went back to his childhood custom of keeping a broomstick beside his bed, just in case.

Resources

Anderson, Geneva. 1939. "Tennessee Tall Tales." *Tennessee Folklore Society Bulletin* 5, no. 3.

Asfar, Dan. 2004. *Haunted Battlefields.* Auburn, WA: Lone Pine Publishing.

Asfar, Dan and Thay, Edrick. 2003. *Ghost Stories of the Civil War.* Auburn, WA: Lone Pine Publishing.

Battle, Kemp P. 1986. *Great American Folklore.* New York: Doubleday.

Bennett, John. 1946. *The Doctor to the Dead: Grotesque Legends and Folk Tales of Old Charleston.* New York: Rinehart.

"Bill Wilson and the Ghost." Pensacola, FL: *Pensacola Gazette*, July 17, 1847.

Botkin, B. A., ed. 1944. *A Treasury of American Folklore.* New York: Crown Publishers.

———. 1965. *A Treasury of New England Folklore.* New York: Crown Publishers.

———. 1953. *A Treasury of Railroad Folklore.* New York: Crown Publishers.

———. 1949. *A Treasury of Southern Folklore.* New York: Crown Publishers.

Brewer, J. Mason. 1972. *American Negro Folklore.* Chicago: Quadrangle Books.

Brown, Alan. 2004. *Stories from the Haunted South.* Jackson, MS: University of Mississippi Press.

Brown, John N. 2002. "History of the Bell Witch." In *Ghosts & Spirits of Tennessee.* Available: http//johnsrealmonline.com/paranormal/bellwitch/adams.

Brown, John N., ed. 2003. "Wampus Cat Encounter." In *Ghosts & Spirits of Tennessee.* Available: http//johnsrealmonline.com/paranormal/submitted/page-03.html.

Burgoyne, Mindie. 2009. *Haunted Eastern Shore.* Charleston, SC: Haunted America.

Chappell, Helen. 1999. *The Chesapeake Book of the Dead: Tombstones, Epitaphs, Histories, Reflections, and Oddments of the Region.* Baltimore, MD: Johns Hopkins University Press.

Childs, Alice. 1929. *American Speech* 5, No. 2. Baltimore: Williams & Wilkins Company.

Coffin, T. P., and H. Cohen. 1973. *Folklore from the Working Folk of America.* New York: Anchor Press/Doubleday.

————. 1966. *Folklore in America.* New York: Doubleday and AMP.

Coleman, Christopher K. 1999. *Ghosts and Haunts of the Civil War.* Nashville, TN: Rutledge Hill Press.

Cox, John Harrington. 1934. "Negro Tales from West Virginia." *Journal of American Folklore* 47, no. 186.

————. 1943. "The Witch Bridle." *Southern Folklore Quarterly* 7, no. 4.

Davis, M. E. M. 1905. *Journal of American Folklore* 17, no. 70. Boston and New York: Houghton Mifflin.

Dorson, R. M. 1973. *America in Legend.* New York: Pantheon Books.

Editors of Life. 1961. *The Treasury of American Folklore.* New York: Time.

Flanagan, J. T., and A. P. Hudson. 1958. *The American Folk Reader.* New York: A. S. Barnes.

Gibbons, Faye. 1997. *Hook Night Moon.* New York: Morrow Junior Books.

Hampton Normal and Agricultural Institute. 1897. *Southern Workman and Hampton School Record* 26. Hampton, VA.: Hampton Normal and Agricultural Institute.

Hendricks, W. C. 1943. *Bundle of Troubles and Other Tarheel Tales.* Durham, NC: Duke University Press.

Hudson, Arthur Palmer. 1928. *Specimens of Mississippi Folk-lore.* University, MS: Mississippi Folklore Society.

Hudson, Arthur Palmer, and Pete Kyle McCarter. 1934. "The Bell Witch of Tennessee and Mississippi." *Journal of American Folklore* 47, no. 183.

Hurston, Zora Neale. 1969. *Mules and Men*. New York: Negro Universities Press.

Ingram, Martin Van Buren, 1894. *An Authenticated History of the Famous Bell Witch*. Available: http://bellwitch02.tripod.com.

"John Wilkins, Sharpshooter." Washington, DC: *The Morning Times,* March 28, 1897.

Kennedy, Stetson. 1942. "Palmetto Country." In *American Folkways,* edited by Erskine Caldwell. New York: Duell, Sloan and Pearce.

Kirkpatrick, Jennifer. 1997. *Blackbeard: Pirate Terror at Sea.* Available: www.nationalgeographic.com/pirates/bbeard.html.

Leach, M. 1958. *The Rainbow Book of American Folk Tales and Legends.* New York: World Publishing.

Lyons, Mary E. 1985. *Raw Head, Bloody Bones.* New York: Charles Scribner's Sons.

Marshall, Theodora. "John Wilkins: Sharpshooter." San Francisco, CA: *San Francisco Chronicle,* Jul 31, 1898.

North Carolina Department of Commerce. 2003. *A Conversation with Blackbeard's Ghost.* Available: http://www.visitnc.com/cst/cst _article.asp?articleid=183&sectiongroupid=13.

Odum, Howard W. 1931. *Cold Blue Moon, Black Ulysses Afar Off.* Indianapolis: Bobbs-Merrill.

Okonowicz, Ed. 2010. *The Big Book of Maryland Ghost Stories.* Mechanicsburg, PA: Stackpole Books.

———. 2007. *Haunted Maryland.* Mechanicsburg, PA: Stackpole Books.

PageWise Inc. 2002. *The Legend of the Wampus Cat.* Available: http: //ksks.essortment.com/wampuscat_rvmr.htm.

Parsons, Elsie Clews. 1917. "Tales from Guilford County, North Carolina." *Journal of American Folklore* 30, no. 116.

Pendered, Norman C. 1975. "Twenty Seven Months of Terror, Treachery and Theatrics." In *Blackbeard!,* accessed August 1,

2003. Available: http://www.ocracoke-nc.com/blackbeard/tales/blcknc0a.htm.

"Pineville Stories: A Night in a Graveyard." Saint Louis, MO: *The St. Louis Republic,* February 17, 1901.

Polley, J., ed. 1978. *American Folklore and Legend.* New York: Reader's Digest Association.

Price, Charles Edwin. 1994. *The Infamous Bell Witch of Tennessee.* Available: http://www.invink.com/x319.html.

———. 2003. "Is the Bell Witch Watching?" In *Linda Linn's Kentucky Home and Ghost Stories,* accessed July 30, 2003. Available: http://members.tripod.com/~lindaluelinn/index-57.html.

Reynolds, Cate. 2013. *The Eerie Tales of a Haunted Eastern Shore.* What's Up? Media. Available: https://whatsupmag.com/news/eerie-tales-haunted-eastern-shore/.

Roberts, Nancy. 2001. *Ghosts from the Coast.* Chapel Hill, NC: University of North Carolina Press.

———. 1988. *The Haunted South.* Columbia, SC: University of South Carolina Press.

Saxon, Lyle. 1945. *Gumbo Ya-Ya.* Boston: Houghton Mifflin.

Thay, Edrick. 2003. *Ghost Stories of the Old South.* Auburn, WA: Ghost House Books.

Young, Claiborne S. "Ocracoke Legend." In *Blackbeard!,* accessed August 1, 2003. Available: http://www.ocracoke-nc.com/blackbeard/tales/blcknc01.htm.

Young, Richard and Judy Dockery. 1991. *Ghost Stories from the American Southwest.* Little Rock: August House Publishers.

Zepke, Terrance. 2005. *Ghosts and Legends of the Carolina Coasts.* Sarasota, FL: Pineapple Press, Inc.

———. 2009. *Lowcountry Voodoo.* Sarasota, FL: Pineapple Press, Inc.

About the Author

S. E. Schlosser has been telling stories since she was a child, when games of "let's pretend" quickly built into full-length stories acted out with friends. A graduate of Houghton College, the Institute of Children's Literature and  Rutgers University, she created and maintains the website AmericanFolklore.net, where she shares a wealth of stories from all fifty states, some dating back to the origins of America. Sandy spends much of her time answering questions from visitors to the site. Many of her favorite emails come from other folklorists who delight in practicing the old tradition of who can tell the tallest tale.

About the Illustrator

Artist **Paul G. Hoffman** trained in painting and printmaking. His first extensive illustration work on assignment was in Egypt, drawing ancient wall reliefs for the University of Chicago. His work graces books of many genres— including children's titles, textbooks, short story collections, natural history volumes, and numerous cookbooks. For *Spooky South*, he employed a scratchboard technique and an active imagination.